VANGUARD SERIES

EDITOR: MARTIN WINDROW

£4·00

ARMOUR OF THE MIDDLE EAST WARS 1948-78

Text and colour plates by

STEVEN J. ZALOGA

OSPREY PUBLISHING LONDON

Published in 1981 by
Osprey Publishing Ltd
Member company of the George Philip Group
12–14 Long Acre, London WC2E 9LP
© Copyright 1981 Osprey Publishing Ltd

ISBN 0 85045 388 7

Filmset in Great Britain
Printed in Hong Kong

Introduction

The troubled lands of the Middle East have seen a major war in each decade since the end of the Second World War, and scores of border incidents, guerilla attacks and retaliatory raids. Unlike most of the conflicts that have afflicted the world since 1945, the Arab–Israeli wars have seen the extensive use of armoured vehicles, sometimes on a scale that rivalled the colossal encounters at El Alamein or Kursk. The aim of this book is to examine briefly the Middle East conflicts from the standpoint of the armoured vehicles used by the combatant states.

At the conclusion of the Second World War Britain decided to extricate herself from the insoluble Palestinian troubles by partitioning the area between its Jewish and Arab inhabitants. The partition plan was to come into effect on 14 May 1948, and its terms were unacceptable to both sides. The Palestinian Arabs called on the help of neighbouring Arab states to help throw the Jews out; and the Jewish settlers, many of them survivors of the recent European horrors, girded themselves for the coming war. Sporadic outbursts grew in intensity as the partition date approached.

Much of the fighting focused around key roads leading to isolated Jewish kibbutz settlements, along which small bands of Arab militia ambushed Jewish supply columns. While protection

should have been afforded by the British garrisons, relations between British troops and Jewish settlers were strained, at best, due to Jewish terrorist attacks on British soldiers. The Jews were forced to rely on their own resources and the clandestine Haganah, the military arm of the Jewish Agency, began assembling an arsenal which included armoured trucks. These were varied in construction, using a wide range of commercial vehicle chassis with armour made from steel boiler-plate, or laminate armour made from plywood or rubber sandwiched between thin metal sheet. Some design standardization eventually took place, but by and large the 'sandwich' armoured trucks were quite a motley collection. The armoured trucks were used to escort unarmoured vehicles to key settlements, and in some heavily-contested areas whole convoys might be made up of armoured trucks. Most of the trucks had some provision for firing ports or firing hatches, but because of British restrictions none could have turrets or permanent weapons of any kind. The heavy weight of the added armour gave them poor performance, and steep hills or heavy loads badly overtaxed their engines and transmissions. Many were lost, with their crews, in the ambushes of 1947 and 1948.

As the outbreak of full-scale war loomed nearer, both sides prepared their arsenals. At the

3

beginning of 1948 the member states of the Arab League held a clear ascendancy in armoured vehicles. While none of the irregular Arab liberation armies had any armoured vehicles to speak of, all of the regular national forces did. The Egyptian Army had been founded in 1936, and in 1937 its first armoured units were formed around a small number of Vickers Mk II medium and Vickers Mk V light tanks. By 1948 none of these were still serviceable, but they had been replaced by a rummage-sale assortment of British hand-me-downs totalling about 200 vehicles. The most numerous types were light tanks like the old Light Tank Mk VI and the M22 Locust airborne

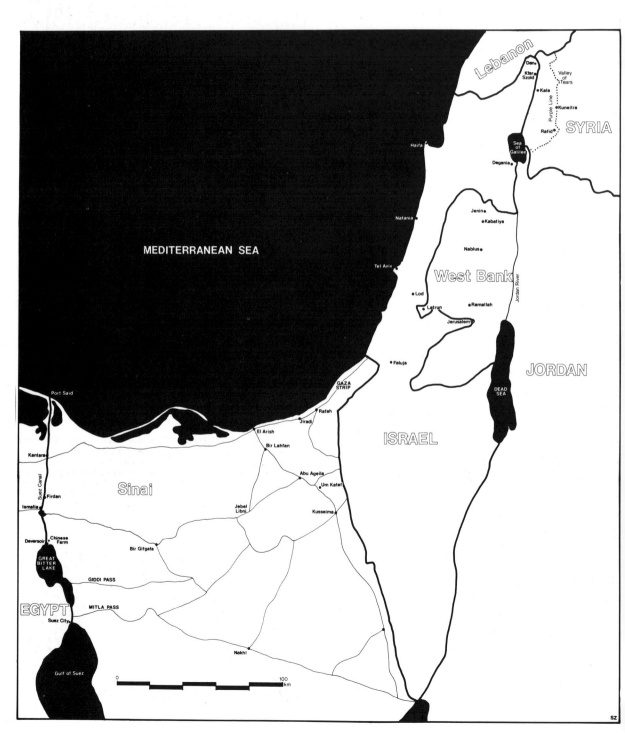

tank. There were a few companies of Valentines and a few Matildas, but the only really modern tanks were Shermans, in roughly company strength. The old desert battlefields were scavenged to come up with a few more, including three unlikely 15cm sIG33 auf Fgst PzKpfw II (Sf), formerly serving with the 707 and 708 sIG Kp (Sf) of the Deutsches Afrika Korps! The Egyptians also fielded a modest selection of armoured cars including the Humber Mk III and Mk IV, the Marmon-Herrington Mk IVF, and some Staghounds. The Egyptian infantry was supplied with 298 Bren carriers, and anti-tank companies had Loyd tracked carriers for towing their 6pdr. AT guns. Egyptian armour was organized along British lines, but in the 1948 fighting it was invariably broken up to support the infantry.

The Syrian Army grew out of French colonial forces, and its armoured units were equipped with left-over French material. The Syrians had one battalion of about 45 R-35 and R-39 light tanks, survivors of the 63ᵉ and 68ᵉ BCC of the Vichy French Forces that had fought Commonwealth units during the Syrian campaign of June-July 1941. The Syrians also had some left-overs from later Free French units; these included some Bren carriers and Marmon-Herrington armoured cars, some *automitrailleuses Dodge* of the Bich type, and a few other armoured cars of French origin. During the fighting in 1948 the tank battalion was broken up into company-sized units of eight to 12 vehicles, and one of these was allocated to each infantry brigade. There were also a small number of self-propelled guns built on improvised chassis, such as 65mm mountain guns on a Chenillette Lorraine 38L, and 25mm anti-tank guns on Bren carriers.

By far the best organized and led Arab armoured contingents belonged to the forces of Transjordan. The Transjordan Frontier Force was equipped with Staghound armoured cars. The Arab Legion had a squadron of Marmon-Herrington Mk IVF armoured cars attached to each of its four lorried infantry battalions. Though smaller than many other Arab forces in overall number of vehicles, the Arab Legion armoured car troops were a force to be reckoned with.

Platoon of Arab Legion Marmon-Herrington Mk IVF armoured cars—the most numerous single type of combat vehicle on the Arab side in the 1948 fighting. A company of Marmon-Herringtons was attached to each infantry battalion of the Legion; the nearest vehicle in this photo is the subject of Plate A2. (Imp. War Mus.)

The small Lebanese Army had a company of older French tanks, probably FT-17s. The Iraqi Army had a battalion of tanks and several armoured car companies. They had ordered some CV-35 tankettes from Italy in 1938, but it is unlikely that any were serviceable a decade later. Most of the equipment used in 1948 was of more recent vintage and of British origin.

The Jews looked to Europe and America when they sought to purchase vehicles to offset the Arab superiority in this area. Many officials in post-war European governments were former Resistance soldiers and were sympathetic to Jewish requests, but could not turn too blatantly

Apart from conventional AFVs, the Arab Legion still had some examples of its six pre-war improvised armoured trucks, ordered in 1939 by Glubb Pasha from the Jaffa firm of Wagner, and veterans of the Mechanized Force operations in Iraq and Syria during the Second World War. The weapon is a Vickers .303 water-cooled machine gun. The Legion's cap badge motif is stencilled, apparently in black, on the sand-painted doors of the truck. (Imp. War Mus.)

deaf an ear to British embargoes and American pressure. Slowly but surely, however, a trickle of 'scrap metal' and 'agricultural implements' bearing a remarkable resemblance to M3 and M9 armoured half-tracks, M3A1 armoured scout cars, and Dodge WC52 ¾-ton trucks began to be routed to Tel Aviv and Haifa. These vehicles were modified by adding additional armour, placing machine gun positions beside the driver, and adding small, multifaceted machine gun turrets on the roof. A deal was also made in France for the purchase of ten old Hotchkiss H-39 light tanks of 1940 vintage which had been used by the 3ᵉ and 12ᵉ Régiments de Dragons of the FFL in 1945.

The primitive 'sandwich' armoured trucks played a major rôle in the intensified skirmishes of April 1948, particularly along the hotly-contested Jerusalem–Tel Aviv road. The British also saw some action. At Rafah in the Gaza Strip a pair of Jewish Chevrolet armoured trucks burned an Arab truck, prompting the garrison there to send out four Comets of the 4th RTR which captured one of the culprits. Most of the rest of the 4th RTR was stationed near the Latrun police station on the West Bank, and on 10 May they witnessed a one-sided encounter between some Arab Legion Marmon-Herrington armoured cars and a few hapless 'sandwich' armoured trucks. The next day, the Jews decided to retaliate by mortaring the police station, which provoked the 4th RTR to send out a few Comets

which blew apart another 'sandwich' truck. Soon, however, the British Army would leave the Arabs and Jews alone to settle their quarrels directly.

The Haganah had many shortcomings in equipment and heavy weapons, but compensated for this by organization, leadership and determination. The Arab League forces were better equipped, but lacked cohesion and co-ordination owing to political rivalries and suspicions among the leaders of the various militias and political dynasties. Although the Haganah had a much smaller population to draw from, it was able to muster an armed force that was not appreciably smaller in real terms than that of all of its Arab neighbours.

1948: The Storm Breaks

On 14 May 1948 Israel came into existence as a sovereign state, and the Arab armies launched their attacks. In the north, along the Golan Heights, the Syrian 1st Infantry Brigade began its advance accompanied by a company of R-35 and R-39 light tanks. On 18 May a combined tank/infantry attack overran some small Jewish settlements outside the two Degania kibbutz compounds, and two days later another attack was launched on Degania itself. The R-35s broke through the wire surrounding the central camp, followed by infantry, and began to blast the defenders' earthen bunkers. They were unprepared for much resistance, but Molotov cocktail attacks and a PIAT anti-tank projector knocked out several tanks. The Syrians turned their attentions to the neighbouring settlements, only to be rebuffed by a recently arrived French Model 1906 65mm mountain gun. Following the fighting the Israelis managed to salvage one R-35 and one R-39 from among the wrecks—Israel's first real tanks. The Syrian 2nd Brigade tried to cross the Jordan on 6 June, but the fords came under fire and the tanks could not wade across. On 10 July a combined tank/infantry attack with artillery support brought this brigade into Palestine, however.

In the Gaza Strip the Egyptian 1st Brigade began its advance up the coast. An infantry attack at Nirim on 15 May, led by Bren carriers, had little effect, but other elements of the Egyptian force continued their advance and assaulted the Yad Mordechai kibbutz. The first two infantry attacks failed, but an assault on 23 May led by Mk VI light tanks and Matildas finally broke into the settlement. A similar attack at Nitzanin on 7 June succeeded in securing this kibbutz, and left the Egyptians in full control of the coast as far north as Ashdod.

The most serious threat to the Israelis loomed in the central area. The Arab Legion was obliged to retire from Palestine on 13 and 14 May, but the next day the armoured cars of two lorried infantry battalions crossed the Allenby Bridge back into Palestine. They quickly reached Jerusalem and seized the key location of Latrun overlooking the road between Tel Aviv and Jerusalem. After seizing the Old City of Jerusalem they fought their way into the Jewish Quarter. Attacks on the New City on 23 May were repulsed when several of the Marmon-Herrington armoured cars were disabled by Molotov cocktails. The Israelis made two assaults on the Latrun positions but were bloodily thrown back by cannon and machine gun fire from the

37mm Humber Mk IV armoured car, one of several types operated by the Egyptian Army in 1948. Note British-style 'C' Sqn. markings in white on turret sides and rear.

armoured cars. In the meantime, to the north, an Iraqi force with an armoured car battalion and a battalion of tanks advanced over the Jordan River and attacked to within ten kilometres of the sea near Natania before being stopped. Israel was nearly severed, both by this attack and by the Egyptian forces to the south around Faluja.

On 11 June a UN ceasefire was imposed, to the relief of both sides. The lack of co-ordination of the Arab attacks had allowed the Haganah to transfer troops to the most vital sector, but Israel had come very near to being overwhelmed. Jeep commandos and truck patrols had blunted many advances. Many of the initial Arab successes were due to Israel's lack of heavy weapons to deal with Arab tanks, but this was soon to be remedied. The Israelis used the lull to reorganize their armed forces, now renamed Zvah Haganah Le Israel (Zahal)—the Israeli Defence Force (IDF). Two mechanized units had been in the process of formation. The 7th Mechanized Brigade received its baptism of fire at Latrun. It was equipped mainly with half-tracks and trucks. The 8th Armoured Brigade was formed under the command of one of Zahal's founders, Yitzak Sadeh. It consisted of the 82nd Tank Battalion commanded by an ex-Polish Army officer, Felix Beatus, and the 89th Mechanized Battalion, a jeep commando unit, commanded by the yet-unknown Moshe Dayan. Before the British had left Palestine the Haganah had managed to acquire, through bribery and theft, a Daimler Mk I armoured car, a Canadian-built GM Otter I recce vehicle and a pair of Cromwell tanks. In addition, one Sherman was pieced together from scrap from a British Army dump near Haifa, and several more Otters of the Police Mobile Force found their way into Israeli hands. The Sherman and two Cromwells formed the so-called 'English company' of the 82nd Tank Bn., and the ten recently-arrived Hotchkiss light tanks formed the 'Russian company'—the titles referring to the most common languages spoken in these polyglot units!

On 9 July the Israelis launched a ten-day offensive. The main threat came from the Arab Legion in the Jerusalem area. The Lydda Airport (today's Lod Airport) was captured by the 82nd Tank Bn., and Dayan's jeep commandos raced

Egyptian Army Humber Mk III Reconnaissance Cars in a pre-war parade. Widely used on patrol duties, these elderly vehicles mounted a light machine gun and a Boys .5 anti-tank rifle—paltry armament by European standards, but perfectly effective against the improvised armoured vehicles on which the Israelis had to rely. (Imp. War Mus.)

ahead to capture Lydda itself, pressing on to Ramle. There were encounters with Arab Legion armoured cars, but this time Zahal had the firepower to handle them. Attacks by the Yiftach Brigade supported by the 82nd Tank Bn. against Latrun were repulsed, however, with a single Legion 6pdr. knocking out several of the Israeli tanks.

In the coastal battles a combined Egyptian attack by Mk VI light tanks and infantry against Negba on 12 July was pushed back, and in subsequent fighting the infantry was supported by Dayan's 89th Bn., brought in after its advance on Ramle. Soon the Zahal units isolated the Egyptians into four pockets around Faluja. In the north little armour was involved, except for some encounters with Syrian armoured cars supporting the operations of Kaukji's Army of Arab Liberation. These included some *automitrailleuses Dodge*, which were Dodge trucks with improvised armour and an old SA.18 37mm gun mounted in a small turret. These were roughly treated by half-tracks of the Israeli 7th Bde. in a battle near Nazareth on 16 July just before another UN ceasefire was declared.

By the time of the July truce the initiative had shifted to the Israelis. Their new armoured units had experienced a fitful initiation, and were being expanded. Just after the Lydda battle the 8th Armd. Bde. began receiving modified half-tracks with 20mm, 2pdr. and 6pdr. guns mounted on them. This gave the half-track infantry units firepower and modest anti-tank capability. Relations between the Arab League countries were at a low ebb, with mutual recriminations flying. Suspicions over Egyptian intentions in southern

Palestine led King Abdullah of the Transjordan to order the Arab Legion over to the defensive. What little co-operation that had existed between the various armies had all but ended. The Egyptian Army now constituted the greatest threat to Israeli plans. Its armoured strength in Palestine now amounted to three Shermans, 132 light tanks (mostly Mk VIs, Locusts and Valentines) and 139 Bren carriers. They were seriously challenged by the Israeli mechanized force, based mainly on improvised armoured cars and half-tracks.

The fighting resumed in October; the Israelis swung over to the offensive in the south while holding tight in the centre and north. Both the 7th and 8th Brigades were shifted to the Southern Command. The 8th took part in the assault at Iraq-el-Manshiyya, but performed very poorly; co-ordination was lacking, and many of the H-39s ran into a tank ditch. The later attack against the Iraq Suweiden Police Station was more successful. The Zahal drive on Beersheba isolated the Egyptian expeditionary forces in the Faluji pocket, and later drives in December and March pushed the Israeli frontier to Eilat on the Gulf of Aqaba before the final ceasefire was imposed by the United Nations.

★ ★ ★

The years that followed the truce were troubled and unstable. A wave of *coups d'état* rocked Syria; the king was overthrown in Egypt, leading to Nasser's rise to power; and young King Hussein assumed the throne of the new Hashemite Kingdom of Jordan, foreshadowing the end of Britain's restraining rôle in the Arab Legion. The Arabs were deeply resentful of Israel, and only their weak economies and internal problems prevented the outbreak of full-scale fighting. Instead, the Arab League subsidized Palestinian terrorist raids in the border areas, which were inevitably followed by Israeli reprisals.

The Zahal emerged from the war proud but wary. The performance of the small tank force had been uninspiring, but Zahal's mechanized units had proved vital to the 1948 victory. Foreign purchases netted more half-tracks, bringing the total to about 300, and purchases of Shermans from various sources gave the Zahal a modest tank force of about 50 vehicles. The 8th Armd. Bde. was disbanded. The 82nd Tank Bn. was shifted over to help form the reorganized 7th Armd. Bde. The 7th Bde. also contained the 79th Mechanized Battalion and the 9th Commandos. The Israeli tank inventory was motley in the extreme; though the Zahal simply called all Shermans 'M1', they in fact consisted mainly of M4A1 (cast hulls) and M4A2 (diesels) armed with everything from 75mm, 76mm and 105mm weapons to a few fitted with old 1914–18 vintage Krupp 77mm field guns.

Israeli Army doctrine at this period was quite conservative, placing the burden of attack on the infantry, with tanks simply to provide support. The bold adventures of a contingent of Shermans from the 7th Armd. Bde. under Uri Ben-Ari in the 1952 Zahal manoeuvres met with a sharp rebuke. At the 1953 manoeuvres this exploit was repeated, much to the delight of Prime Minister Ben Gurion, who was present. Ben Gurion also happened to be Defence Minister, and the sight of infantrymen fleeing before the Shermans convinced him that more tanks had to be acquired from Israel's meagre defence budget. At the time the French government was increasingly angered by Egyptian support for Algerian guerillas, and so decided to encourage Israel militarily. Israeli tankers were allowed to train at the French cavalry school at Saumur, and sales of Shermans and new AMX-13 light tanks were permitted. (Ironically, the Israelis found Syrian students at Saumur as well, owing to France's long-standing ties with her old colony.) The French sold the Israelis 100 AMX-13s, 150 M3 half-tracks, 60 *Obusier automoteur de 105 Modele 50* (self-propelled 105mm howitzers on an AMX-13 chassis), and 60 Sherman tanks, bringing Israeli tank strength to about 200 vehicles. This permitted the formation of two reserve armoured brigades, the 27th and 37th.

The British helped in the re-equipment of the Egyptian Army. The old Mk VIs and useless M22s were scrapped, and Valentines relegated to training. About three battalions of Sherman Mk 3s (M4A2) were provided, along with 200 Archer self-propelled 17pdr. anti-tank guns. In 1955, 41 Centurions from Britain and the sale of some Shermans with FL10 turrets from France brought

Bren carriers were used in quantity by Egypt; the heavy weapons platoon of each infantry brigade usually had 25 of them, and many were captured by Israel, like this one on 19 October 1948 in the Negev Desert. Note green/white/green Egyptian roundel on side, and ahead of it the hastily chalked insignia of Zahal's Southern Command.

Egyptian tank strength to about 200 vehicles. Nasser had been negotiating with the Western Powers to help Egypt finance a major dam on the Nile at Aswan as part of his economic modernization plan. To keep his feet planted in both camps he arranged a major arms deal with Czechoslovakia, sponsored by the Soviet Union. This included 230 tanks, mostly T-34/85s but also including some IS-3s; 200 BTR-152 armoured troop carriers; and 100 SU-100 self-propelled guns. This permitted the formation of the 4th Armoured Division, consisting of the 1st and 2nd Armoured Brigade Teams and the 2nd Infantry Brigade. The armoured brigades each had a single tank battalion, a motorized infantry battalion on BTR-152s and a battery of SU-100s. This deal backfired on Nasser, as it enraged the Western countries, leading the US and Britain to withdraw from the Aswan Dam project. This rebuke led Nasser to nationalize the Suez Canal to help pay for the dam, and precipitated an international crisis.

The French were displeased with Nasser for his meddling in the touchy Algerian crisis, and the Suez affair was the last straw. In August 1956 a joint Anglo-French military team began to lay plans for a seizure of the canal coded Operation 'Hamilcar'. After political objections were raised, the focus of the assault shifted from Alexandria to Port Said, and the plan was re-named 'Musketeer'. It was set to go into operation in September, but was postponed to draw in Israel. The Israelis were becoming increasingly concerned over

Zahal workshops produced standardized armoured car conversions for several common vehicles. In the foreground of this parade is a car built on an M3A1 Scout Car chassis, with completely altered rear hull configuration and an added turret; standard armament was two MG.34s and a Besa MG. Behind are two GM Otter 1 armoured cars with new enlarged turrets. Note 7th Armd. Bde. insignia carried on small plates, on the fender of the M3A1 and centrally at the top of the radiator on the Otters. A small blue and white Star of David device also seems to be painted on the door of the M3A1. Such insignia were usually limited to parade use.

Egyptian-sponsored raids from the Gaza Strip. Israeli participation in the form of an attack into the Sinai would provide the Anglo-French with an excuse to disembark at the Suez Canal as a 'peace-keeping force' between the unruly Egyptians and the Israelis. The Israelis would strike first on 29 October, to be followed by Allied air strikes on Egyptian airfields on 31 October, and finally an Allied landing at Port Said on 5 November.

Neatly re-marked Bren carrier in Israeli service sports the three arrows of Southern Command, a Zahal serial, and on the left front fender, as viewed, some kind of heraldic unit insignia.

In addition to the 60 Shermans purchased from the French in 1955 the Israelis now requested a further 100 up-gunned Shermans and 200 half-tracks, which arrived by LST near Haifa in July 1956. These were called M50 Super-Shermans by the Israelis, and consisted of M4s with their old 75mm gun replaced by a VO1000 75mm high-velocity gun like that used in the AMX-13. This was designed to deal with the Egyptian's new T-34/85s. The conversion necessitated a new gun mantlet and a rear turret extension, carried out at the Atelier de Bourges in France. The tank battalion of the 37th Armd. Bde. was the only Israeli unit to be re-equipped with this new type for the 1956 fighting.

The Israelis did not entirely trust their British allies, and decided to limit their first two days' fighting to a parachute drop near the mouth of the Mitla Pass and an infantry probe towards Kusseima. Should the air strikes not materialize on 1 November, these forces could be pulled back and explained away as a retribution raid. The three armoured brigades were not scheduled for involvement until D-Day + 2. The Israeli phase of the operation was codenamed 'Kadesh'.

The Egyptians had two major armoured units in the Sinai, and several smaller ones. The 3rd Armd. Bn., attached to the 3rd Inf. Div., was headquartered at El Arish on the coast. It consisted of three companies of Shermans (16 tanks each), a training company of unarmed Valentines, three recovery Shermans, and a trio of

Sherman 'dozers. Two of the companies were kept as divisional reserves at El Arish, while one was stationed with the 5th Inf. Bde. at Rafah in the Gaza Strip.

One of the tank companies at El Arish was equipped with French-supplied M4/FL10s. These were Shermans with their regular turrets removed and replaced by FL10 turrets like those used on the AMX-13. They were roughly equivalent to the Israeli Super-Shermans, and were built by Batignolles-Chatillon. The rest of the battalion's vehicles were Sherman Mk 3s (M4A2s with 75mm guns and VVS suspension). In addition, there were at least four Archer SP anti-tank batteries, each with 11 guns. The 78th and 94th AT Batteries were stationed at the Abu

the night of 29/30 October. By noon the next day it had advanced up to Egyptian positions at Um Katef on the way to the key road junction at Abu Ageila, but was quickly halted when two or three tanks and three half-tracks were knocked out by Archers of Capt. M. D. Zohdy's 78th AT Bty. on the heights. The 7th Armoured pulled back and decided to try to get to Abu Ageila through the back door. In the meantime, responsibility for dealing with the Egyptian positions astride Um Katef-Um Shehan was left to the infantry of the 4th and 10th Brigades. They soon lost more half-tracks to fire from the Archers, ZiS-2 57mm anti-tank guns and 25pdr. field guns. On 31 October the 7th Armd. Bde. entered Abu Ageila from the rear, but was challenged by a formation of

Ageila garrison, and the other two were at El Arish and Rafah. When the fighting broke out, the 78th AT Bty. stationed at the Um Katef-Um Shehan crossroads was reinforced with three more Archers, bringing its strength up to 14. The Egyptian infantry formations in the Sinai had about 300 Bren carriers.

Israel's first major armoured action was the capture of Lod (Lydda) airport in July 1948; here, the 'Russian company' of the 82nd Tank Bn., 8th Armd. Bde. rest after the battle, with one of their ten H-39 tanks in the foreground, and an armoured car built on a Dodge ¾ ton chassis and a second tank in the background.

1956: Operation 'Kadesh'

The Israeli 7th Armd. Bde., commanded by Col. Ben-Ari, consisted of the 82nd Tank Bn. (M4A1 Shermans with VVS suspension and 76mm guns), the 79th Tank Battalion (AMX-13s), a battalion of half-track infantry and one of lorried infantry. It was not scheduled for operations until 1 November on the explicit instructions of the Chief of Staff, Gen. Moshe Dayan. However, this order was 'misunderstood', and it took part in the advance on Kusseima with the 4th Inf. Bde. on

Shermans and Archers sent from the 3rd Armd. Bn. in El Arish. The Egyptian tanks did not enter range before they were stopped by an air strike. They remained at long range and tried to shell the Israelis. At this time an unco-ordinated attack was launched by Archers from the bypassed Um Katef positions, supported by infantry in Bren carriers. This was thrown back. By evening Abu Ageila was in Israeli hands, and the 7th Armd. Bde. was ordered to prepare to send a detachment further west to the Jebel Libni crossroads to prevent an attack by the Egyptian 1st Armd. Bde. Team on the Israeli paratroops near Mitla.

Although the crossroads at Abu Ageila had been taken, the defensive positions in front of it had not. The 37th Armd. Bde. was hastily sent into action. Its Sherman battalion and AMX-13

Probably the most potent Israeli AFV conversion—an M9 half-track with a British 6pdr. anti-tank gun mounted leads a column in the Negev, December 1948. This particular vehicle served with 8th Armd. Bde.; see Plate B1. Behind it is a Scammell wrecker.

squadron had not yet reached its two infantry battalions, but the brigade was sent on a night attack without them. The half-tracks were soon badly shot up, and the brigade commander killed. The next day, 1 November, the Anglo-French air forces began striking Egyptian air-fields and, fearing that their forces would be cut off, Egyptian High Command ordered all Sinai units to withdraw. The Archer units and the infantry around Um Katef carefully withdrew to El Arish without the Israelis realizing it. In a bitter sequel, columns of both the 7th and 37th Armd. Bdes. approached Um Katef the next day from opposite directions in the hope of finally finishing off the enemy positions; they mistakenly took each other for Egyptians, and the 7th Armd. Bde. knocked out eight friendly tanks before the mistake was realized.

On 30 October Sharon's 202nd Parachute Brigade, including its AMX-13 squadron, made a forced advance to link up with part of the brigade that had been air-dropped near the eastern end of the Mitla Pass. After fighting their way through several Egyptian garrisons they arrived in the evening, and spent most of the night in violent hand-to-hand fighting along the banks of the Mitla Pass after trying to extricate a motorized patrol that had wandered too far. The brigade was subsequently ordered southward to Sharm-el-Sheikh.

The anticipated drive by the Egyptian 1st Armd. Bde. Team on the Jebel Libni crossroads never materialized, and so the Israeli 7th Armd.

Bde. moved westward towards Bir Gifgafa, where the Egyptian tanks were pulling out. A short firefight with an Egyptian rearguard left eight T-34/85s blazing, but further down the road two Israeli tanks were lost, and the column halted for the night. On 2 November the advance continued and another rearguard detachment consisting of a platoon of T-34/85s and some SU-100s was roughly treated, leaving four T-34s and four SU-100s behind. Many of the rest of the Egyptian brigade's vehicles were lost to air strikes during their withdrawal to the Suez Canal.

On the morning of 1 November the 27th Armd. Bde. of Col. Haim Bar-Lev joined the 1st (Golani) Brigade in an attack on the Gaza Strip. The 27th had a motorized infantry battalion and four tank squadrons each of about 13 tanks. One of the squadrons had AMX-13s, another M4A1s (76mm guns with HVSS suspension), and the remaining two had new M50 Super-Shermans. One of the Super-Sherman squadrons was de-tached to fight alongside the Golanis. The 27th Armd. Bde. pushed past Rafah and out westward along the coast, driving for El Arish. The Egyptian withdrawal in accordance with the order of 1 November was quite precipitous, and the 27th had no time to count the booty while on their way to the Canal. On the morning of 2 November they were only a dozen kilometres from the Suez Canal when they were ordered to stop.

During Operation 'Kadesh' the Israelis knocked out or captured 26 T-34/85s, one T-34 com-mand tank, six SU-100s, 40 Sherman Mk 3s, 12 M4/FL10s, 15 Valentines, 40 Archers, 60 BTR-152s, three Sherman ARVs, three Sherman 'dozers and 283 Bren carriers. Total Israeli casualties had been 172 killed, 817 wounded and about 30 tanks and half-tracks knocked out in combat.

Operation 'Musketeer'

The Anglo-French landings were due to begin on 5 November. It was feared that either Egyptian Centurions or IS-3 Stalins with Russian or Egyp-tian crews would contest the landings, so the invasion force was amply provided with armour. The British had assembled a Buffalo unit, desig-nated No.1 Landing Vehicle Troop RAC, equipped with LVT Mk IIIs. The 6th Royal Tank Regt., with Centurions, was due to disembark with the force landing on 6 November. Among the French units, M47 Pattons and AMX-13s of the 8ᵉ Dragons were scheduled to land as part of the 7ᵉ Division Méchanique Rapide. LVT-3 amtracs were to take part in the amphibious landings; and in the 10ᵉ Division Parachutiste the 1ᵉʳ REP (1st Foreign Legion Paratroopers) had an attached squadron of AMX-13s from the 2ᵉ REC (2nd Foreign Cavalry). In the event the only Egyptian armour encountered were four SU-100s detached from the 53rd Arty. Bty. of the 1st Armd. Bde. Team then fighting the Israelis in Sinai. They were disposed of by British paratroopers air-dropped on 5 November.

★ ★ ★

The 1956 war concluded amidst international political furor. The collusion of the British, French and Israelis was all too apparent, and political pressure, particularly from the USA, forced an Allied withdrawal. The war profoundly effected the political complexion and alliances of the Middle East, even if it did not alter national frontiers. Their experience impressed the Israelis with the combat potential of armoured formations, and altered their tactical perceptions. While the Armoured Corps had entered the war a poor second to the infantry, the reverse would thereafter be the case.

The Egyptians showed great skill in the defensive battles around Abu Ageila, but their counter-attacks were half-hearted and poorly executed, and the withdrawal order of 1 November led to a humiliating rout. The 1956 war left the Arab states no better disposed towards Israel's existence, but ill-prepared to contest it. Further hostilities were confined to border incidents on the Golan Heights and the West Bank. Continued political tension led to a gradual enlargement of the armies facing Israel.

In 1956 the British officers who had trained and, to a decreasing extent, led the Arab Legion were ordered out of Jordan at short notice, and the Legion became the Jordan Arab Army. At

'M1' Shermans (M4A1 76mm, Wet) of Zahal's 7th Armd. Bde. replenishing fuel and ammunition near Jebel Libni during Operation 'Kadesh', 1956.

Israeli AMX-13 with FL10 turret, still carrying the blue-cross-on-white air ID marking used in the 1956 campaign. Note also the bridging circle on the left fender as viewed; and Russian-style padded tank helmets.

this point the fledgling Royal Jordanian Armoured Corps consisted of the 1st and 2nd Armoured Car Regts. (with Marmon-Herrington Mk IVs and 6pdr. Mk IVFs); the 3rd Tank Regt. (with two sabre squadrons each of about 20 Charioteers, and a squadron of Archers), and several companies of Archers attached to the National Guard, totalling about 24 guns. In spite of the ill-feeling caused by the ungracious dismissal of Glubb Pasha in 1956 Britain still retained ties with Jordan, and in the early 1960s consented to sell King Hussein some 90 Centurions. At the time of the 1967 war they equipped a battalion of the Royal Guards Brigade and the 10th Tank Battalion. Jordan's relative moderation and pro-Western stance led the USA to offer arms and, beginning in 1964, deliveries began. The first vehicles received were M47 Pattons, which were used to form the new 40th Armoured Brigade. When newer M48s became available some of the M47s were transferred to the 12th and 47th Tank Bns., which were attached to infantry divisions in time of war. The arrival of the M48s also allowed the formation of a second armoured brigade, the 60th. In all Jordan received about 140 M47s and 160 M48s, as well as about 36 self-propelled M52 105mm howitzers which formed the 8th Royal Artillery Bn. and two other artillery battalions. Mechanized infantry companies were equipped with M113 APCs, of which 210 were purchased. The old Marmon-Herringtons were put out to pasture, and the Charioteers were sold off to Lebanon. Small numbers of Saracen and Ferret armoured cars were used for security and patrol duty.

Throughout the 1950s France remained Syria's primary military sponsor. The Syrians received Panhard 178B armoured cars, and when France began to increase its sales to Israel in 1953–54 the government felt compelled to offer the Syrians something more potent in order to maintain a balance. They were offered some reconditioned German vehicles of Second World War vintage including PzKpfw IV Ausf.Hs, and a few StuG IIIs and Panzerjäger IVs. (There are reports that a few Panthers were supplied, but this has not been confirmed, and no such tanks were encountered by the Israelis.) A series of *coups d'état* pushed Syria steadily to the political Left, and French influence was replaced by that of Soviet Russia.

In the early 1960s the USSR began supplying Syria with T-34/85s. These, together with some of the old Panzer IVs, were involved in the 'Water War' beginning in November 1964. The Syrians tried to disrupt Israeli agriculture by diverting the Jordan River. The Israelis responded with artillery fire and air strikes against the dam site, and the Syrians in their turn began harassing Israeli farm tractors in the valley below the Golan Heights with tank fire. The Israelis brought up some 105mm Centurions of the 7th Armd. Bde., and eventually the Syrians were silenced. Following these incidents the Soviets consented to supply more modern weapons, and the first shipments of T-54s began to arrive to supplement the T-34s and SU-100s already delivered. The Syrian 14th and 44th Armd. Bdes. were formed with T-54s, T-55s and some T-34/85s; about eight tank battalions, to be attached to infantry brigades in wartime, were formed with T-34s and Panzers. The SU-100s were attached to anti-tank companies in the armoured and mechanized brigades, and the 17th Mechanized Bde. was formed with BTR-152 APCs. By 1967 Syria had about 750 tanks and 585 APCs.

The war put Egypt solidly in the Soviet camp, and large quantities of military aid were forth-

The standard Egyptian APC in 1956 and 1967 was the BTR-152, an armoured derivative of the ZIL-151 truck. This is the BTR-152 VI version, characterized by unusual external tyre pressure regulators on the wheels.

coming. This allowed Egypt to prosecute its war in the Yemen, and to hand some armour over to the Yemeni Republican Army and the Palestine Liberation Army. In 1956 the first shipment of Czech-built T-34/85s and 120 new T-54s arrived and were used to rebuild the 4th Armd. Div., routed in the Sinai campaign. In 1962–63 more T-34s were received, along with another 130 T-54s. In 1965–67 another 160 T-54s and T-55s were received, along with about 25 IS-3M Stalins and 50 amphibious PT-76s. According to some sources a further 30 heavy tanks were supplied, including some IS-4s and T-10s, but it is unclear whether or not these ever left the hands of the Soviet advisory teams. Large numbers of APCs were also supplied, including BTR-40, BTR-50, BTR-60 and BTR-152 versions. The major SP artillery type supplied was the SU-100, of which 18 served in the anti-tank company of each armoured brigade. Small numbers of ZSU-57-2 anti-aircraft tanks, ASU-57 airborne SPs and ISU-152 heavy assault guns were also provided. Egypt's old Shermans and a dozen M4/FL10s were supplied to the 20th PLA Division in the Gaza Strip, totalling about 50 vehicles. An effort to encourage indigenous production of military vehicles started with the Walid APC, a small armoured truck somewhat resembling the BTR-40.

The 1956 victory impressed Israel with the need for large, mobile armoured formations. Encouraged by their experiences they began to contemplate the use of larger tactical formations called *ugdas* (divisional task forces), which would consist of a mixture of armoured brigades with mechanized or infantry brigades, depending upon circumstances. To facilitate these new tactics the number of tank brigades was increased from three to nine between 1956 and 1967.

Equipment for the new units came from a variety of sources. The acquisition of T-54s by Egypt forced the Israelis to look for more modern battle tanks. Britain agreed to sell Israel Centurion Mk IIIs and Mk Vs, and subsequently provided new L7 105mm guns to replace the less effective 20pdrs. in the elderly vehicles. The Centurion would become famous in 1967, but Zahal's early experience of it was unfavourable. The crews held very disparaging views of its mechanical reliability in desert conditions. Some of the difficulties were overcome by Ordnance Corps modifications; and reforms introduced from 1964, when Gen. Israel Tal took command of the Armoured Corps, cleared up the inadequate maintenance procedures which lay at the heart of the problem. By 1967 the bugs had been ironed out, and the 'Water War' convinced many Israeli tankers of the quality of their Centurions. By this time Israel had about 250 of them, the majority with 105mm guns.

The second new tank to be adopted was the American M48 Patton. The USA refused to sell weapons to Israel directly, but as a sideline to the reparations agreements between Israel and the Federal Republic of Germany the USA secretly agreed to the transfer of M48A2C Pattons from the Bundeswehr to Zahal. These transfers lasted from 1960 to 1964, totalling about 200 vehicles before press leaks put a stop to the shipments. The USA agreed to continue direct arms shipments to Israel on a limited basis.

With only a handful of Centurions and Pattons actually in service in 1962, Zahal became anxious when it learned of another shipment of T-54s from Russia to Egypt. This tank presented a serious problem for the M1s, M50s, and AMX-13s which made up the bulk of the Israeli tank force at that time. A crash programme to mount an even heavier gun in the old Sherman was begun. French and British guns were tried, but only cracked the vehicle's armour. The Atelier de Bourges in France, which was at that time developing a new 105mm gun for the AMX-30

tank, came up with a more modest version designated VO980 which they succeeded in mating to a T23 Sherman turret by modifying the mantlet and adding an extended rear bustle. They co-operated with Israeli Ordnance in modifying about 200 old M1s (M4 Shermans with 75mm and 76mm guns) by adding the new VO980 gun and a SAMM CH23-1 hydraulic system. The weight of the modification taxed the old engines of the Shermans, so it was decided to modify the rear engine decks to allow the use of a more powerful Cummins VT8-460 liquid-cooled 460hp diesel engine. For better flotation on desert sand the old VVS suspensions were replaced by HVSS and wider tracks. The resulting vehicle was named M51HV, or Isherman (Israeli Sherman). In 1967 the majority of these served in three battalions; one in Col. M. Aviram's brigade, one in Col. M. Zippori's brigade, and one in the 10th (Harel) Brigade. The Israelis also began to up-arm their M48s with the 105mm gun, but only one company in the two battalions using Pattons in 1967 had this feature. The 105mm Centurions and Pattons served mostly with Southern Command on the Sinai Front.

During the 1956 war Israeli mechanized units were supported by batteries of 105mm M50 SP howitzers on AMX-13 chassis. Heavier support was required, so about two battalions of M7 Priest SP 105mm howitzers were acquired from France. These were essentially similar to the war-time version, but the French had upgraded the howitzer to standards comparable to the American M101. The Israelis had purchased French *obusiers de 155mm Mle 1950*, and now desired an SP version for armoured brigades. The French firm of EFAB developed a drastically modified version of the Sherman to mount these howitzers on a rear platform. Israeli Ordnance adopted this basic design and incorporated many of their own features, particularly with regard to armour layout and automotive redesign. Several batteries of these SP guns were ready in 1967; they were usually referred to as Model 1950 SP howitzers. The Ordnance Corps also began

mounting Soltam M65 120mm mortars in half-tracks to provide fire support and illumination fire for armoured brigades.

Zahal's mechanized infantry usually depended on supporting tank units for anti-tank defence, but late in the 1950s two half-track tank destroyers were developed for this task. The French developed a kit for mounting a new DEFA F1 90mm anti-tank gun on old 6pdr. carriages. The Israelis bought a number of these and carried the idea one step further by developing a *portee* mount for the 90mm gun on their half-tracks. Unlike the arrangement of the conventional *portee*, it allowed the dismounting of gun, trunnions and shield from the carriage, and their mounting separately on the vehicle. The carriage was towed behind, and the gun could be removed from the half-track and replaced on it for use as a conventional towed weapon. (Many anti-tank companies ignored this rather cumbersome system, and simply left the carriages at home!) The second tank destroyer design consisted of a half-track with a light armour roof over the rear compartment on which was installed a battery of SS-11 wire-guided anti-tank missiles.

1967: The Six-Day War

The outbreak of war in 1967 was the culmination of a series of political acts which convinced Israel that its Arab neighbours were planning to turn their usual inflammatory rhetoric into violent action. Egypt forced the withdrawal of the UN peace-keeping force from the Sinai, and threatened to blockade the Straits of Tiran. Reconciliation between Jordan, Egypt and Syria after a decade of intermittent mutual abuse raised the serious prospect of a co-ordinated attack. Egypt reinforced her troops and tanks in the Sinai. In retrospect it is doubtful if Nasser seriously planned to launch an assault on Israel; but given the hysterical fervour of his public pronouncements, and the movement of Arab troops on her borders, it is hardly surprising that Israel reacted to his provocation by staging a pre-emptive attack. Israeli strategy is governed by the perilous geographical facts. Israel is small, and very narrow in the area containing its major population centres. A defensive war on the European model is impossible, since the territory in which to carry out a defence in depth is lacking. Israeli military doctrine has therefore rested on offensive operations carried out by mobile forces from the onset of hostilities, and this of course led to the cultivation of armoured and air forces. The plan in 1967 was to eliminate the main threat, Egypt, by wiping out its Sinai garrison, and then to turn on Syria to exact retribution for border incidents over the past decade. (Until the last minute the Israeli government attempted to avoid hostilities with Jordan, and had King Hussein not been sucked into war by Nasser's deliberate deceit the course of recent history might have been very different.) This plan stretched the capabilities of Israel's mobile forces to the limit; success depended on the usual lack of co-ordination among the Arab states, and the usual skill and determination of Zahal's troops.

The Sinai Front

Since 1956 the proportion of armoured and mechanized brigades in Zahal had grown at the expense of infantry brigades. The majority of the units facing Sinai in 1967 were armoured or mechanized. The typical Israeli armoured brigade was built around two tank battalions, usually with about 50 tanks apiece, each broken down into three or four companies, each of four three-tank platoons. These two battalions were supported by at least one battalion of half-track infantry, plus a scouting company and supporting brigade artillery. The armoured brigades were formed into *ugdas* along with mechanized or infantry brigades; these *ugdas* varied in composition. During the 1967 war there were four of

them: three in the Sinai, and one in Jordan and, later, Syria. Israeli security regulations are still so unyielding that the actual designations of most of the armoured brigades are not known, so in this account brigades are referred to by their commanders' names.

The strike force in northern Sinai, Ugda Tal, was commanded by the Armoured Corps chief, Gen. Israel Tal. It consisted of Col. Shmuel Gonen's 7th Armoured Brigade; Col. Menachem

The 89th Anti-Tank Bn. of Egypt's 4th Armd. Div. was equipped with Czech-built SU-100 SP guns.

Aviram's Armoured Brigade; Col. R. Eitan's half-track Paratroop Brigade; and Col. Uri Barom's Mechanized Reconnaissance Task Force. The 7th Armd. Bde. comprised Maj. Ehud Elad's 79th Tank Bn. with Pattons, and the 82nd Tank Bn. with Centurions. The Aviram Armd. Bde. had a battalion of AMX-13s and another of Isherman M51HVs. Barom's Task Force had a battalion of Pattons and a few companies of AMX-13s.

To the south of Tal was Ugda Yoffe, consisting of an armoured brigade of Centurions under Col. Isska Shadni, and another, also with Centurions, led by Col. Elhanan Sela. Further south still the third 'division', Ugda Sharon, had one infantry brigade, and an armoured brigade commanded by Col. Mordechai Zippori with one battalion of Centurions and one of Ishermans. The *ugda* also had a recce battalion of AMX-13s; but the paratroop brigade which should have completed it was removed and sent to the Jordanian front before fighting began.

The plan was for Ugda Tal to strike through the key Rafah Junction positions in the Gaza Strip, and to push on to El Arish on the coast. Ugda Yoffe was to skirt through the wastes south of Tal and to prevent the reinforcement of El Arish. Sharon would take the key Abu Ageila positions which had caused Israel such problems in 1956, and would then push on to the Mitla and Giddi Passes. Besides the three *ugdas* there was an independent armoured brigade commanded by Col. Albert Mendler positioned in the Negev as a counterbalance to the Egyptian Shazli Force.

The most bitterly contested action of the 1956 war was the determined defence of Um Katef near the key Abu Ageila crossroads by two Egyptian independent anti-tank companies of 17pdr. Archer SPs, which cost the Israelis dearly in men and equipment.

Egypt's garrison in the Sinai consisted of four infantry divisions, an armoured division, and an armoured task force. The 20th PLA Div. in the Gaza Strip had a battalion of old Shermans, about a dozen of which were M4/FL10s. The 7th Inf. Div., located behind it from Rafah Junction along the coast to El Arish, had the support of about 70 tanks including some 30 IS-3M heavies. There was also a company of SU-100s, large numbers of BTR-152 APCs, and, guarding El Arish airstrip, a battery of ZSU-57-2 anti-aircraft tanks. The 2nd Inf. Div. was positioned in the Abu Ageila defence triangle with 88 tanks in support, mostly T-34/85s, and an additional force of dug-in SU-100s. The 3rd Inf. Div. was in reserve around Jebel Libni, with a similar complement of armour.

In the Kuntilla-Nakhl region was the 6th Mechanized Div., with which served the 1st Armd. Bde. (T-54s and T-55s) and the 125th Armd. Bde. (partly equipped with IS-3M heavies). The usual composition of Egyptian

armoured brigades at the time was three tank battalions each of 31 tanks. The 4th Armd. Div., around Bir Gifgafa, was equipped almost entirely with newer vehicles including T-54s, T-55s and PT-76s. It had two armoured brigades, and a mechanized infantry brigade with a further tank battalion; in all the 4th Armd. Div. had some 250 tanks and SP guns and about 150 APCs. The Shazli Force, supporting 6th Mech. Div., had about four tank battalions with around 120 tanks. In total, the Egyptian forces in the Sinai had at their disposal about 930 tanks when war broke out.

The Israelis launched the war on 5 June 1967 with a series of spectacularly successful air strikes on Arab airfields, which gave the Israeli Air Force almost complete air supremacy during the subsequent fighting. Ugda Tal quickly broke into Khan Yunis with 79th Tank Bn. leading. The combined efforts of 7th Armd. Bde. and Barom's Force overwhelmed the Rafah area defences, leading to the destruction of some 20 T-34/85s dug in there. The Centurions of 82nd Tank Bn. pressed on to Sheikh Zuweid, where a further ten T-34s were knocked out. Barom's Patton battalion, supporting the paratroopers' assault on the Egyptian 7th Inf. Div. at Rafah, became heavily involved with supporting Egyptian armour and knocked out 15 IS-3M Stalins, a pair of T-34/85s and an SU-100. Fighting around the Egyptian positions near Kafr Shan continued into the afternoon, and in a later tank duel Barom's Pattons destroyed two more Stalins and five T-34/85s. One IS-3M attacking an un-escorted paratroop unit was disabled by a carefully-aimed rifle grenade which was ricocheted off the open turret hatch into the fighting compartment.

Meanwhile an advance company of 82nd Tank Bn. had pushed through the Jiradi positions largely unopposed; but when the rest of 7th Armd. Bde. arrived the Egyptians had re-established their defences, and put up a stiff fight. A head-on attack at Jiradi left the commander of 79th Tank Bn. dead and three company commanders wounded. That evening a night attack broke through the Egyptian defences and linked up with a Centurion company on the El Arish road. The tanks were nearly out of fuel, but when re-supplied on the morning of 6 June the brigade took El Arish. In a pitched battle on the city outskirts a Patton company from Barom Force took the airstrip after overcoming the T-34s and ZSU-57-2 anti-aircraft tanks stationed there.

Along the southern edge of Ugda Tal's advance, Aviram's two tank battalions became involved in a confused battle with 20 Stalins and a similar number of T-34/85s in the sand dunes south of Sheikh Zuweid. By evening the Egyptian force had been defeated, and Aviram's Armd. Bde. joined the drive on El Arish.

Ugda Yoffe set off on the morning of 5 June through the trackless desert between Tal in the north and Sharon in the south. The area was considered impassable by the Egyptians and was not heavily defended. The terrain was treacherous, and the Centurions moved out in low gear on their slow march westwards. By that evening Shadni's Armd. Bde. was south of Bir Lahfan and came under ineffectual enemy shelling. One battalion was ordered to hold the road against any Egyptian attempt to push armour up against Tal's southern flank at El Arish. At nightfall on the 5th an Egyptian armoured brigade and a mechanized brigade began approaching from Jebel Libni, and a firefight ensued. The Israelis turned on their searchlights and knocked out several T-54s, but this became hazardous when the enemy began firing at the lights, which were turned off or shot out. The Egyptians did not exploit the advantage of their tanks' infra-red searchlights. The following morning the stand-off ended. In the valley below the Israeli position 65 T-54s could be seen, nine of them burning from the night's fighting. Air strikes were called in and further gun duels ensued. The Egyptians pulled back leaving 28 wrecks behind them.

Ugda Sharon had the prickly task of overcoming the defences at Abu Ageila. Most of the Egyptian 2nd Inf. Div. tanks—about 88 T-34/85s—were positioned several kilometres behind the main defences. After the grim experience of 1956 the Israelis carefully prepared a multi-pronged night assault. Paratroopers were dropped behind the Egyptians to silence the artillery pits; an Isherman battalion drew fire from the frontal positions, while a tank/infantry team swarmed across the supposedly impassable dunes north of

Port Said, 22 December 1956; Centurions of the British 6th RTR during the UN-negotiated withdrawal of Anglo-French forces. Note black horizontal turret band, and white 'H' roof marking. (United Nations)

the defences to strike the unprotected left flank. The Egyptian positions were overwhelmed, and Zippori's tanks prepared for an Egyptian counter-attack. A fierce night tank battle followed, but the Egyptians withdrew before daybreak rather than face the inevitable Israeli air strikes, leaving about 40 T-34/85s behind. The Israelis had lost about 19 tanks in this action, but had secured the most formidable defensive belt in the Sinai. As this encounter took place the Mendler Armd. Bde. moved out towards El Thamad and Nakhl to prevent the Shazli Force from attacking Ugda Sharon.

On the morning of 6 June Gen. Amer, the Egyptian commander-in-chief, sent telegrams to his divisional and brigade commanders ordering them to withdraw to the Suez Canal. It was a fatal decision, and all the more surprising in view of the disastrous effects of an identical order in 1956. Some Egyptian officers convinced themselves that the Israelis could not have carried out their devastating air strikes without American collusion, and feared that another seaborne assault on the Canal might be in the offing. Equally troubling was the speed with which key Sinai defences had fallen. No plans were sent out for a fighting withdrawal; it was to be a straightforward flight in the face of the enemy. By the time saner counsels prevailed on Amer to rescind the order the damage had been done; the Egyptian Army was in headlong retreat towards the Canal, and resistance crumbled.

Throughout 6 June the three Israeli divisions

M3A1 Scout Car of Yugoslavian patrol unit serving as part of the UNEF monitoring force stationed in the Sinai at the conclusion of the 1956 war. (United Nations)

pushed on westwards. The largest armoured encounter flared up between an Egyptian rearguard at Jebel Libni and tanks of the 7th and Shadni's armoured brigades. The Egyptians won some time, at a cost of 32 tanks. By this point it had become evident to the Israelis that the Egyptians were in uncontrolled retreat. They decided to launch a breakneck drive to cut off as much of the Egyptian Army as possible before it reached the Suez Canal. Ugda Tal was assigned the Kantara road along the coast and the vital Ismalia road in central Sinai. Yoffe's Centurion brigades would take the key Mitla and Giddi Passes, and Ugda Sharon would cover the southern escape routes. The plan was to send small forces racing ahead to block key roads long enough for the main bodies of the divisions to arrive and deal with the encircled enemy.

Tal concentrated most of his armour along the Ismalia axis. The 7th Armd. Bde. attempted to envelop the Egyptian 4th Armd. Div. around Bir Gifgafa, but succeeded only in trapping a single brigade which had become entangled with Aviram's Shermans. By nightfall Aviram's AMX-13 battalion was far in advance up the Ismalia road when two battalions of T-54s from across the Canal came racing towards it in a vain attempt to relieve 4th Armd. Div. positions which had, in fact, already been abandoned. The lightly-armoured AMXs were outnumbered two-to-one, and their 75mm guns were nearly useless against the T-54s' frontal plates. Several Israeli tanks and half-tracks were lost in a matter of minutes, although a few T-54s were knocked out by audacious flank shots. As the AMXs were being forced to retreat a company of Centurions from 82nd Tank Bn. finally arrived, and in a

brief firefight the Egyptians lost ten T-54s and were forced to fall back.

Shadni's Armd. Bde. took the point for Ugda Yoffe, battering its way through the fleeing Egyptian columns all afternoon. More and more of the Centurions dropped out as they ran out of fuel, and by the time the column arrived at the approaches to the Mitla Pass at 6pm on 6 June only nine tanks were left, of which four were being towed for lack of fuel. These few tanks, along with some of the brigade's half-tracks, hastily set up ambushes, and their positions were soon enveloped by the fleeing Egyptian columns. Israeli aircraft joined the fray with bombs and rockets. In the battles of the night of 6–7 June Shadni's unit was nearly overrun, and resorted to using captured Egyptian equipment when its own ammunition ran low. Finally, more Centurions of the Sela Brigade arrived, and by morning the Egyptians gave up their attempts to escape through the Mitla Pass. Thousands of burned-out tanks, trucks and troop carriers littered the roads leading into the defile.

Ugda Sharon had advanced toward Nakhl, where they found the abandoned tanks of the Egyptian 125th Armd. Bde., including some 30 heavy IS-3M Stalins. On the morning of the 7th the combined forces of the Zippori and Mendler Armd. Bdes. began a four-hour battle with rearguards of the retreating Shazli Force, destroying about 60 tanks and numerous other vehicles. That same morning, in the north, the 7th Armd. Bde. fought its way through several rearguards and reached the Suez Canal opposite Ismalia. Parts moved north along the Canal to link up with 'Granit Force' near Kantara. The Centurions of Sela's Brigade had begun pushing through the rearguard defences inside the Mitla Pass, but ran into stiff opposition. A night attack, with searchlights and guns blazing, finally broke through. By mid-day on 9 June the three *ugdas* had all linked up and had begun picking up stragglers. A United Nations ceasefire came into effect that evening. In their drive through the Sinai the Israelis had lost 122 tanks; while this was fairly modest in view of the magnitude of the victory, the especially severe losses among tank and unit commanders were serious for an army the size of Zahal. Egyptian losses were cata-

strophic. Of the 935 tanks in the Sinai at the beginning of hostilities Egypt had lost more than 820: 291 T-54s, 82 T-55s, 251 T-34/85s, 72 IS-3M Stalins, 51 SU-100s, 29 PT-76s, and around 50 Shermans and M4/FL10s. Losses in APCs and other types of armoured vehicle had been equally severe.

Israeli M1 Shermans on manoeuvres in 1961 display the more conspicuous markings adopted as a result of experience in 1956. The hull chevron and barrel stripe indicate 1st Coy., the '2' on the turret indicates 2nd Platoon, and the large Hebrew letter *beth* ahead of this indicates the second tank in the platoon. Note also white band, edged black, on turret roof as air ID symbol. These markings proved excessively prominent and were later reduced in size. Less evident is a small white tactical marking on the differential housing in the form of a 'V' in a broken square, the meaning of which is unknown.

The Jordanian Front

The Jordanian front erupted on 5 June. Initial Israeli thrusts were conducted by infantry and paratroopers with very modest armoured support: two Sherman battalions were assigned to the capture of Jerusalem, while the 10th Mech. Bde.—the Harel Bde.—drove north of the city with a mixed battalion of M50 Super-Shermans and 20pdr. Centurions, and a battalion of AMX-13s. Jordanian infantry contested these advances with characteristic stubbornness; but in their first armoured attack three Jordanian tanks were knocked out by recoilless rifle fire when they attempted to take Mt. Scopus. The M48 Pattons of the Jordanian 60th Armd. Bde. attacked Israeli forces on the Ramallah–Jerusalem road, but lost several tanks to the Harel Bde.; a fast lunge by this Israeli formation cut off the rest of the 60th Bde., and many more Pattons were lost to Israeli air strikes. By the time it fought its way out the following day the 60th Bde. had only six tanks left.

The attacks into the central part of the West Bank were followed by an assault by Ugda Peled, composed of one infantry and two armoured brigades. The brigade led by Col. Moshe Bar Kochva had three tank battalions totalling about 100 tanks, mostly M50 Super-Shermans and M51HV Ishermans, and one battalion of half-track infantry. The armoured brigade led by Uri Ram had two tank battalions with Centurions and AMX-13s. The Bar Kochva Bde. launched its attack on Jenin and Ya'Abad on the afternoon of 5 June, running into the M47 Pattons of the Jordanian 47th Tank Bn.; the fighting lasted all day, and the Jordanians were able to claim 17 Shermans knocked out in a well-executed envelopment. The Jordanians were finally pushed back that night, and their 40th Armd. Bde. was rushed to the scene. The M48s of this brigade's 4th Tank Bn. took up positions overlooking the roads in the Kabatiya area, while the 2nd Tank Bn. covered the area to the south. Part of 4th Tank Bn. was hit by Israeli half-track 120mm

The M51HV Isherman was one of the fastest tanks in Israeli service in 1967, and proved quite effective despite the antiquity of the basic vehicle. These are believed to be tanks of 4th Pln., 2nd Coy. of the Isherman battalion of Col. Zippori's armoured brigade serving with Ugda Sharon in the 1967 Sinai campaign; there is reason to believe that the half-circular sign with the Hebrew letter *shin* inset was a temporary tactical insignia assigned to the whole *ugda*.

mortars, and while trying to evade their fire ran into a minefield, forcing them to abandon some of their tanks. The survivors of this detachment of 4th Tank Bn., amounting to some 28 M48s, got mixed up with a recce patrol of Israeli Shermans and a close-range duel followed. The Jordanians fell back that night after losing 15 tanks.

The remaining elements of 4th Tank Bn. had been brought under fire by Centurions of Ram's Armd. Bde., but at long range, with inconclusive results. An evening air strike cost Jordan another four Pattons.

An early morning drive by Ram's Armd. Bde. towards Nablus knocked out 21 Pattons. The other detachment of 4th Tank Bn. in the northern positions facing Bar Kochva's Armd. Bde. was hit by another 120mm mortar barrage, and the Israelis claimed 22 tanks knocked out. With this, the Jordanian 4th Tank Bn. had been almost totally destroyed. The bulk of the 2nd Tank Bn. in the Nablus area was pinned down between Ram's two tank battalions; in the fighting which followed a single AMX-13 was credited with destroying seven M48s. The remainder of the 2nd Tank Bn. was hit by Bar Kochva's tanks near Silat Edh Dhahr. In all, only eight M48s of the 40th Armd. Bde. escaped over the Jordan River.

During the fighting the Jordanians lost 179 tanks as well as many M113s and M52s; but they had cost the Israelis 112 tanks disabled, both by tank fire and anti-tank artillery.

The Syrian Front

Apart from artillery duels and small-scale skirmishes the Syrian front was quiet for the first days of the war. After the Arab defeats in the Sinai and on the West Bank, Syria would have been agreeable to a ceasefire on 8 June; but Israel was determined to put a stop to the Syrians' ability to shell settlements from the commanding positions on the Golan Heights, and so planned an assault on 9 June. Col. Albert Mendler was brought up from the Sinai to command another armoured brigade equipped with one battalion of Centurions and one with a mixture of M50 and M51 Shermans. In addition, both Bar Kochva's and Ram's Armd. Bdes. were brought up from the West Bank. Besides these units there were a number of independent tank battalions attached to the five infantry brigades taking part in the assault.

The Syrian armoured force consisted of the 14th and 44th Armd. Bdes., with several additional battalions of Panzer IVs, T-34/85s and T-54s attached to Syrian infantry formations in the area, and some SU-100s of anti-tank companies. Many of these tanks and SPs were well dug-in with only their turrets exposed.

The initial assault at mid-day on 9 June was spearheaded by Mendler's Armd. Bde. preceded by bulldozers. The mountain slopes from Kfar Szold up the Golan Heights were an awesome natural barrier, and the Syrians had fortified them with minefields and emplaced anti-tank guns. The 'dozers and Mendler's Centurion battalion took heavy casualties as they fought their way up the slopes, but finally the crest was reached. Some confusion over the direction of the rocky trails caused the brigade to go into their attacks on the heavily-defended road junctions of Zaoura and Kala split up; by the time the latter was taken the Sherman battalion was down to only three operable tanks. Ram's tanks assaulted the Syrian positions from Gonen, and reached the oil pipelines running along the border.

On 10 June the Syrian General Staff decided

that it was futile to try to contest the advance further, since Israel had already overcome the most serious defences: they therefore tried to obtain a cease-fire agreement at the United Nations. Israel made sure that her forces were in firm control of the Golan Heights before agreeing. Bar Kochva's Armd. Bde. entered the fray near Dan, and by the afternoon the Israelis held the key town of Kuneitra. The ceasefire took effect that evening.

Although there were no large-scale tank-vs-tank clashes on the Golan Heights to compare with those in Sinai, Zahal lost more tanks there in two days of fighting than in either of the other two theatres. The advance up the difficult mountain tracks had cost about 160 tanks, or nearly a third of those committed. In contrast, Syria lost 73 T-34/85s, PzKpfw IVs and T-54s; seven SU-100s; and a few old StuG IIIs.

★ ★ ★

The Six-Day War was a stunning victory for Zahal. The vital role played by the Armoured Corps assured it of a central place in post-war planning. The spectacular victories in the Sinai led to a tendency to underrate mechanized infantry and to place too much confidence in all-armour formations. Nevertheless, steps were taken to replace the vulnerable half-tracks which had been in use since 1948. Some M113s were captured from Jordan, and when the USA reversed its arms shipment policy Israel purchased a number of these. There had never been any doubt that the AMX-13 was outdated, and heavy casualties in AMX units now led the Israelis to pull these out of regular battalions and to limit them to service in scouting units. The M51HV had proved to be a useful expedient, showing up quite well against more modern Jordanian M47s and M48s. The older M50s were mustered out gradually and their chassis used for SP guns, such as a new type mounting Soltam's 160mm mortar.

Several hundred repairable T-54s and T-55s had been captured; while Israel did not judge these as entirely satisfactory due to their small internal size and other factors, many were re-manufactured and entered Israeli service as the 'Ti-67'. The peculiar transverse engine mounting

To give tank battalions close support, Zahal Ordnance developed this M9 half-track mounting the 120mm Soltam mortar. Perhaps their most surprising successes came on the Jordanian front, where they were credited with destroying a number of Pattons of the Jordanian 40th Armd. Bde. in the Six-Day War.

arrangement made powerplant replacement extremely difficult, but the Israelis did substitute a new L7 105mm gun for the Soviet D-10T 100mm gun on some of these tanks. Many small changes were made to the vehicles, and Soviet radios and machine guns were replaced by US types. The remainder of these tanks kept their old 100mm guns, since Israeli magazines had acquired large quantities of ammunition for them. Other captured equipment, as well as some of the older Israeli equipment, was sold off to raise funds to purchase more modern items. Egyptian Walids and BTR-152s were widely issued to Israeli border police for patrolling the newly-captured territories.

The workhorses of the armoured brigades, the

The obsolescence of the AMX-13 was painfully emphasized in several encounters with Egyptian T-54s in 1967, and it was later used only for reconnaissance. Like many Israeli AFVs of that campaign, this AMX carries its tank and platoon markings on a canvas sheet lashed to the turret.

Centurion and Patton, were both well regarded, though neither was wholly without its critics. The Centurion was liked for its armour protection, but it was slow, and its powertrain and engine were inadequate. Following the war these components were replaced by the Continental diesel and transmission used in the American M60A1. This version was sometimes called the 'Ben Gurion' in the popular press, but Zahal simply called it the modified Centurion. The M48 was faster and more reliable than the Centurion, and after the war the programme to up-gun it with the L7 105mm was completed. At the same time the Continental diesel was retro-fitted to the M48, to improve its performance and simplify logistics. One of the Patton's most objectionable features was its cupola. Israeli commanders were taught to fight 'head out' for better visibility; and the high cupola, on an already-high tank, exposed them to unnecessarily heavy casualties. Many M48s had their cupolas replaced by a low-profile version like that used on the initial models of this series. Even on those M48s and M60s not modified in this way, it was usual to see the cupola machine gun removed and replaced by a .30 cal. Browning mounted outside for ease of use.

The Israelis generally preferred the slower, more heavily armoured British tank designs. Several Chieftains were in Israel at the time of the 1967 war, but these were in British hands and saw no fighting. The Israelis would have been happy to adopt it as their new main battle tank had a change in political climate in Britain not made this impossible. The AMX-30 was evaluated, but rejected due to its thinner armour. Israel finally settled on the M60A1, and began to receive it in quantity in 1970. Among the most popular acquisitions from the USA were the M107 and M109 SP guns: the M107, with its long 175mm gun, was especially popular for its long-range performance in the artillery duels which broke out during the so-called War of Attrition.

The War of Attrition

The fighting had hardly ceased when sporadic border incidents again broke out. In March 1968 Israel launched a major border raid at Kerama in Jordan in retaliation for guerilla raids in the West Bank. That year the War of Attrition broke out along the Suez Canal, with Israel and Egypt trading artillery barrages and commando raids; it proved to be a costly and aggravating war for both countries. The most violent fighting of this period occurred in September 1970 in Jordan. The Palestinian guerillas, encamped there in great strength, overplayed their hand, and began to pose a direct threat to the authority of King Hussein's government. Hussein called in fiercely-loyal Bedouin battalions of his army to curb their power; this they did in short order, but Hussein's purge of the PLO forces prompted Syria to try an invasion of northern Jordan in support of the Palestinians. Syrian units included the T-54s of the 9th and 88th Armd. Bdes., but they discovered—as Israel had already learned—that Jordan's tankers were the best in the Arab armies. The Jordanian 40th Armd. Bde., backed by Hawker Hunter jets, sent the Syrians reeling back over the frontier.

Syria became the main base for the PLO and the most vocally militant of the Arab states. Soviet Russia agreed to rebuild the Syrian Army after its embarrassing defeats of 1967 and 1970, and set about the task in the grand manner; Syria received the T-62 before Moscow's Warsaw Pact satellites, and was even supplied with the sophisticated BMP infantry combat vehicle. The Syrians relegated their T-34/85s to static defence, or converted them into improvised SP guns by mounting new 122mm D-30 howitzers in place of the turret.

Syria formed her new armoured divisions along Soviet lines. The two divisions each had two armoured and one mechanized infantry brigades supported by an artillery brigade with towed guns and truck-mounted Katyusha rockets. The armoured divisions had priority for the T-62s, and their mechanized infantry used the BMP. Each armoured brigade had three tank battalions with 30 or 31 tanks apiece, and each mechanized infantry brigade had its own tank battalion. Syria's three infantry divisions each had an organic tank brigade, and the two independent infantry brigades had an organic tank battalion each. While the armoured divisions were brought to full strength, the infantry formations varied. The 5th Inf. Div. had its full complement of

1. **Hotchkiss H-39, Israeli 82nd Tank Bn.; Lydda airport, 1948**

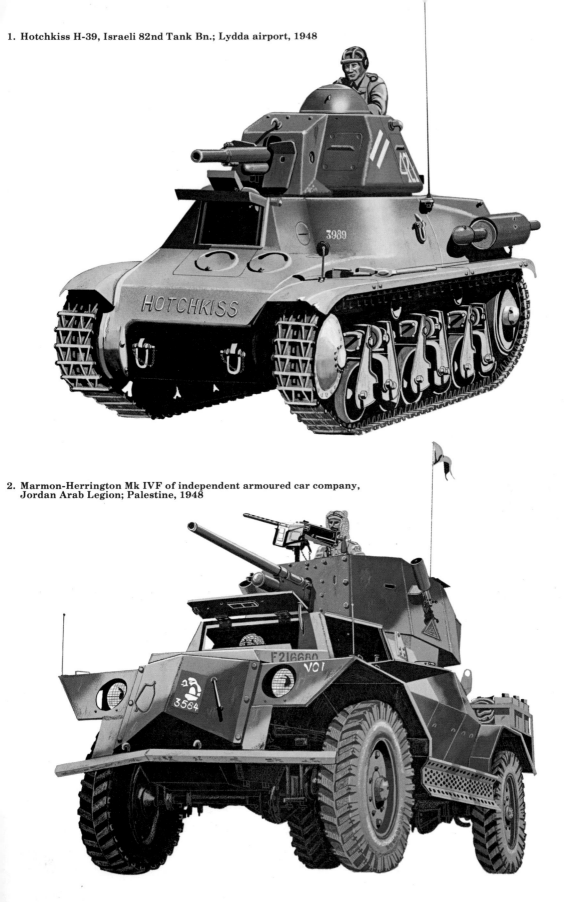

2. **Marmon-Herrington Mk IVF of independent armoured car company, Jordan Arab Legion; Palestine, 1948**

A

1. M9 half-track (6pdr.), Israeli 82nd Tank Bn.; Negev, 1948

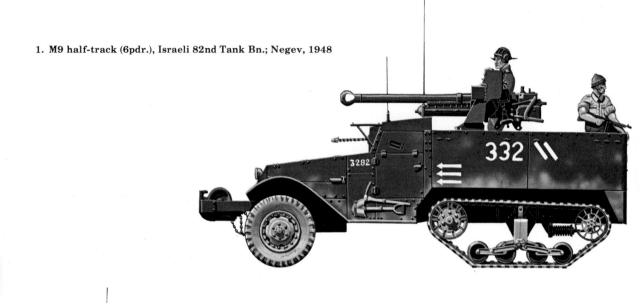

2. Archer 17pdr.SP, Egyptian independent anti-tank company; Sinai, 1956

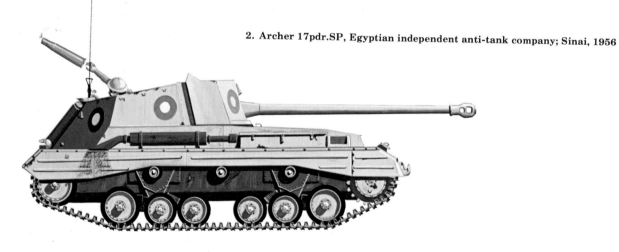

3. White M3A1, Israeli Military Border Police, 1954

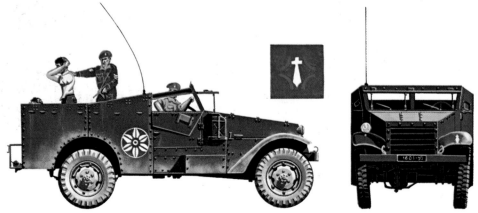

B

1. M1 Sherman (M4A1 76mm), Israeli 7th Armd.Bde.; Sinai, 1956

2. AMX-13, French 1erREP; Port Said, 1956

C

1. T-55, unit unknown, Egyptian Army; Sinai, 1967

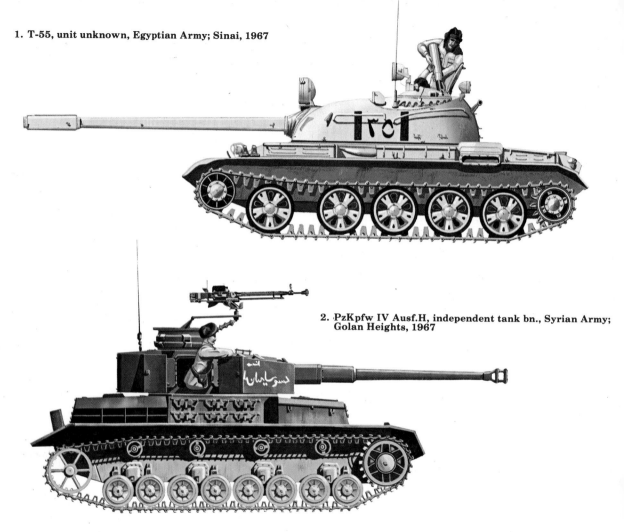

2. PzKpfw IV Ausf.H, independent tank bn., Syrian Army; Golan Heights, 1967

Arab AFV insignia — see Plates commentary.

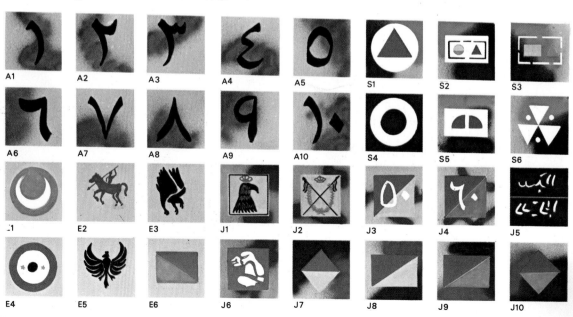

A1 A2 A3 A4 A5 S1 S2 S3

A6 A7 A8 A9 A10 S4 S5 S6

E1 E2 E3 J1 J2 J3 J4 J5

E4 E5 E6 J6 J7 J8 J9 J10

D

1. M48A2C Patton, 79th Tank Bn., Israeli 7th Armd.Bde.,Ugda Tal; Sinai, 1967

2. M47 Patton, 40th Armd.Bde., Royal Jordanian Armd.Corps; West Bank, 1967

E

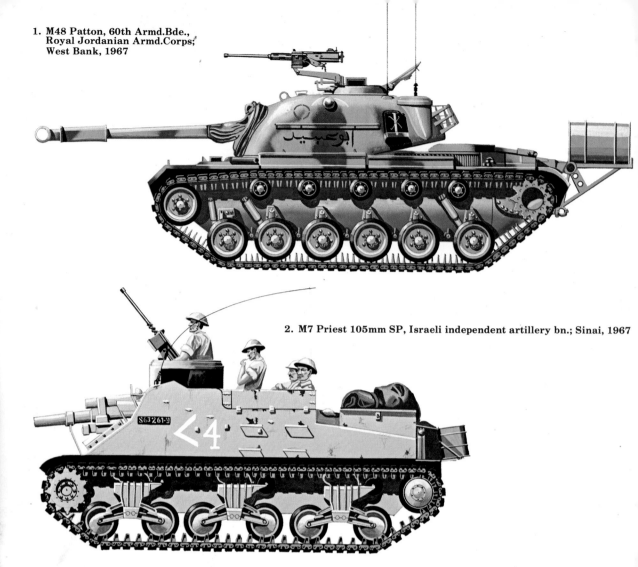

1. M48 Patton, 60th Armd.Bde.,
   Royal Jordanian Armd.Corps;
   West Bank, 1967

2. M7 Priest 105mm SP, Israeli independent artillery bn.; Sinai, 1967

Israeli AFV insignia — see Plates commentary

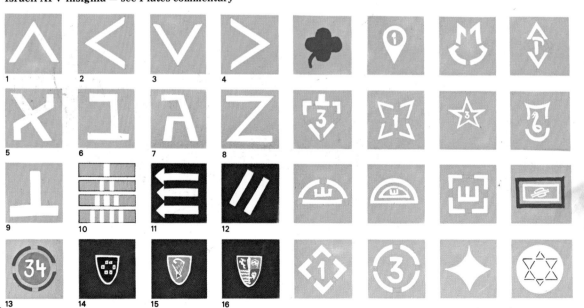

F

1. M113A1, Lebanese Falangist militia; Beirut, 1975

2. T-62A, unknown armoured brigade, Syrian Army; Golan Heights, 1973

G

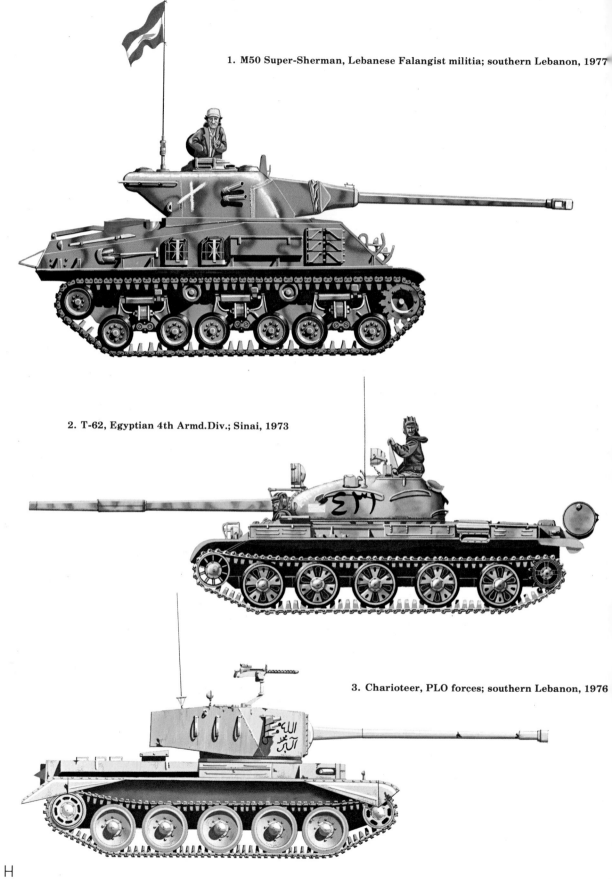

1. M50 Super-Sherman, Lebanese Falangist militia; southern Lebanon, 1977

2. T-62, Egyptian 4th Armd.Div.; Sinai, 1973

3. Charioteer, PLO forces; southern Lebanon, 1976

H

tanks, but the 7th had only 80 per cent establishment, and the 9th only around 50 per cent.

Syria also had four independent tank brigades, including the Assad Republican Guard Brigade, with T-62s, which defended the capital. Anti-tank battalions within each infantry division each had 27 BRDM-2 (9M14M) Malyutka tank destroyers in three companies, and two companies of towed 107mm recoilless rifles. The ZSU-23-4 Shilka anti-aircraft tank would prove a real scourge in 1973; many of Syria's 27 anti-aircraft companies were equipped with this new vehicle, six per company.

The Egyptian Army also received generous aid, which allowed the complete re-equipment of the gutted 4th Armd. Div., the formation of a new armoured division, and full-scale mechanization of several infantry divisions. Egypt received 1,260 T-54s and T-55s between 1967 and 1973, and 400 T-62s between 1971 and 1973. New troop carriers comprised 550 BTR-60s and BTR-152s, 150 BMPs, and, from Czechoslovakia, 200 each OT-62s and OT-64s. They also received 200 BRDM-2 Malyutkas. The most novel items purchased were a wide range of specialized bridging and amphibious vehicles suitable for a large-scale crossing of the Suez Canal; among these were several companies of GSP tracked ferries, used to transport tanks across waterways.

Few weapons had so much impact on the style of tank warfare in 1973 as the anti-tank missiles supplied to the Arabs. The simplest of these was the unguided, shoulder-launched RPG-7, which was lavishly issued to infantry assault teams. More novel was the small, man-portable Malyutka wire-guided missile (NATO codename 'Sagger'). This came packed in a small 'suitcase' containing the disassembled missile, a simple launcher, and the 'joy-stick' fire control assembly. The team would set up the missile and launcher in one spot and the firing controls and periscopic sights a short distance away. The missile operator would locate a tank in the sight, fire the missile, then guide it on its way to the target with the joy-stick by keeping his eye on both the target and the flares in the tail of the missile. The Malyutka was more primitive than the American TOW, but it was small, mobile, and available in large numbers. It also came mounted on the BRDM-2

armoured car in an elevating platform with six launch rails.

This type of weapon was not new to the Middle East. The Israelis had the similar SS-11 in use in 1967, but did not care for it; and the Egyptians had an earlier version, the 3M6 Schmel (AT-1 Snapper) in service in 1967 mounted on UAZ-69 jeeps, called the 2P26 'Baby Carriage'. Neither type had any impact on the fighting of 1967; the difference in 1973 lay in the quantity available and the training of the crews. Apart from these cheap anti-tank weapons, Russia also supplied Syria and Egypt with sophisticated anti-aircraft missile systems, which had a direct bearing on the inability of the Israeli Air Force to mount major close-support strikes in the early days of the Yom Kippur War.

1973: The Yom Kippur War

By autumn 1972 Anwar Sadat of Egypt was convinced that the only way to break the unfavourable diplomatic stalemate was to launch another war against Israel. The aim of the war would be to recover the whole Sinai, but Egypt cherished no illusions about the difficulty of achieving this, and even a sizeable foothold east of the Canal was considered worth the cost. It took little to win over Syria to the plan. Timing was dependent on the speed with which Russia supplied necessary aid, weather factors, and the readiness of the Israelis. Major deception plans were put into effect to convince the Israelis that there had been a quarrel with the Russians, and to camouflage the build-up of forces on the Golan Heights and the Suez Canal. The date picked was 6 October 1973, since Zahal would be disrupted by the Yom Kippur religious holiday, and might be expected to assume that the Arab forces would likewise be distracted by the Ramadan festival. The attack was set for Saturday afternoon, the 6th, when Israeli soldiers on the Golan would have to fight with the sun in their eyes, and when nightfall would give the Egyptians long hours of respite to throw their bridges over the Canal before the Israeli Air Force could interfere.

The Syrian Front

The deception succeeded, and Israel was caught almost completely off guard by the attacks of 6 October. The wariness of some Israeli officers had led to elements of the veteran 7th Armd. Bde. being assigned to duty on the Golan Heights, and this one example of foresight proved to be a major factor in foiling Syrian plans. The defence of the 'Purple Line' along the Heights had been assigned to one infantry and one armoured brigade, the 188th Barak Armd. Bde.; this latter had four battalions totalling 90–100 tanks supported by 44 105mm and 155mm SP guns. The 7th had some 105 tanks, but only a part of the formation was committed when the Syrians struck. In their favour the Israelis had carefully laid out concealed fire positions, minefields and tank traps to channel any Syrian attack into 'killing grounds'. Nevertheless, some 200 Israeli tanks faced about 1,260 Syrian tanks and several hundred other armoured vehicles.

The 7th Armd. Bde. was scattered along the northern edge of the Purple Line from the Lebanese border to Kuneitra, enjoying the advantage of very rough terrain. The Barak Bde. defended 40km of better tank country south of Kuneitra to the Jordan frontier. The Syrians struck with their three infantry divisions in the lead: the 7th, 9th and 5th Inf. Divs., reading

Czech-built T-34/85 disabled near Ein Fite in the Banias area in 1967; Syrian T-34s were modified by the addition of large stowage boxes on the hull sides, and a large and rather cumbersome mount for the DShK machine gun on the cupola. Like most Syrian tanks of 1967 this one is painted dark green overall, with a dedication on the turret—'In memory of Hermiz Yunis Butrus'; most such markings commemorated heroes of the 1948 war. A red turret triangle does not show up in this print—see Vanguard 14, *The T-34 Tank*, Plate D. (Joseph Desautels)

In 1967 Zahal experimented with French SS-11 wire-guided AT missiles mounted on jeeps and, as here, on roofed-in half-tracks. Their performance was disappointing, which added to the Israelis' shock at the success of the more sophisticated Malyutka missiles used by Egypt in 1973.

north to south. Behind them, ready to exploit success, were the 1st and 3rd Armd. Divs. and the independent tank brigades. Each infantry division had some 200 tanks under command, which were used in the first waves.

The Syrian attacks of 6 October were held by the Israeli tankers, despite unusually intense Syrian artillery fire. The first enemy waves to reach the tank ditches were roughly thrown back; subsequent waves which breached the ditches by using tank bridge-layers and tractors were halted by local Israeli counter-attacks. In the night battles which followed the 7th Armd. Bde. managed to hold on to its positions in the north; but in the south the more exposed defences of the Barak Bde. were overrun with heavy losses. The 46th Tank Bde. of the 5th Syrian Inf. Div. broke through near Rafid, and by dawn they overlooked Israeli settlements on the Sea of Galilee.

The Syrian command quickly pushed the 1st Armd. Div. and 15th Mechanized Bde. into the gap. Elements of the Israeli 79th Reserve Armd. Bde. were thrown into action piecemeal to link up with surviving tanks of the Barak Bde. in a desperate attempt to plug the rent torn in the Purple Line. Twenty tanks faced 600; by afternoon of the 7th many had been knocked out either by tank fire or by roving RPG-7 teams. Three more reserve armoured brigades—the 14th, 17th and 19th—were rushed to the scene

under command of Gen. Dan Laner, and were driven into the fray company by company as available, with little chance to form coherent units. By the night of Sunday 7 October these measures seemed to be working; no further breakthroughs were reported, and Israeli units were coalescing.

Single-handed, the 7th Armd. Bde. clung to its positions on the slopes overlooking the 'Valley of Tears', where 130 Syrian tanks already lay burning. The amazing success of 7th Armd. Bde. led Israeli commanders to concentrate their efforts in the south; but by the afternoon of Tuesday the 9th, the threadbare survivors of this brigade were nearly cracked apart by unrelenting assaults from the Syrian 7th Infantry. The handful of Israeli tanks still running had been pushed back from several key crests and were nearly out of ammunition when 13 tanks of the reconstituted Barak Bde. arrived on the scene and tore into the Syrian flank, disabling 30 tanks. In the low ground below the 7th Armd. Bde. positions lay the smouldering wrecks of 260 tanks of the Syrian 7th Inf. Div. and the Assad Republican Guard. Over 200 other armoured vehicles such as bridge-layers, BMPs and BRDMs also littered the valley. Of the original strength of 105 tanks, 7th Armd. Bde. had seven surviving runners. As impressive as the brigade's record had been in past wars, little in their history could match their desperate four-day defence of the Purple Line north of Kuneitra.

On the morning of Wednesday 10 October the Israeli counter-offensive opened. The rebuilt 7th and 188th Armd. Bdes. moved forward north of Kuneitra, while Laner's 240th Armoured Ugda —19th, 20th and 79th Armd. Bdes.—advanced in the south. Although bled white in the difficult fighting of the previous few days, the Syrians were still full of fight and put up a tenacious rearguard defence. On 12 October Laner learned of a major attack building up on his right flank. This was the Iraqi 3rd Armd. Div., come to help the Syrians, with Jordan's 40th Armd. Bde. not far behind. Inexplicably the Iraqis halted, giving the Israelis the time to lay a massive ambush before the attack developed the next day. Hit from both sides, the Iraqis lost 80 tanks before retreating. An unco-ordinated attack on 18 October by the Iraqis and the Jordanians left 60 Iraqi and 20 Jordanian tanks burning on the field. This was the last major armoured confrontation on the Syrian front.

The Suez Front

The Egyptians struck on Saturday afternoon, 6 October, and implemented a brilliantly conceived and executed crossing of the Suez Canal. The lightly held fortifications of the Israeli Bar Lev line were submerged in artillery fire, and the

Among the AFVs used by Syria in the Water War and the 1967 Golan Heights campaign were old, reconditioned German PzKpfw IVs and StuG IIIs. This StuG III has a horseshoe-shaped armour shield added in front of the cupola. See also Vanguard 18, *The Panzerkampfwagen IV.* (Bryan Perrett)

Israeli Air Force was kept away by a thick protective belt of SAMs. Amphibious assault teams crossed in OT-62s and BTR-50s followed by more infantry as soon as pontoon bridges were erected. The first units to be rushed forward were the tank-hunter squads, who set up their Malyutka missiles along trails that Israeli tanks would be likely to use to relieve their besieged fortifications. The first major armour encounter occurred when PT-76 amphibious tanks and BTR-50 troop carriers of the 130th Marine Brigade attempted to storm the entrances to the Mitla and Gidi Passes. Their thin armour gave them little protection against the 105mm guns of Israeli tanks in the area, and they were quickly blown apart. The Egyptians began pushing heavier tanks over the waterway by using the GSP tracked ferries.

At the time of the Egyptian assault the major Israeli armoured formation in the forward portion of the Sinai was Gen. Albert Mendler's 252nd Armoured Ugda. This consisted of the 14th Armd. Bde. commanded by Col. A. Reshev,

Egypt's attack over the Suez Canal in 1973 was greatly aided by a range of Soviet amphibious equipment such as this GSP heavy ferry. These came in pairs, one having a pontoon which folded to the left, the other to the right. Once in the water and linked along their free sides these ferries were buoyant enough to support a tank; they were used to move tanks over the Canal in the initial assault, before large pontoon bridges could be erected. This vehicle bears the number '62' in Arabic. (Joseph Desautels)

the 401st Reserve Armd. Bde. commanded by Col. Dani Shomron, and the 460th Reserve Armd. Bde. commanded by Col. Gabi Amir. The 14th Armd. Bde. was the first sent into action, but the tactics that had been so successful in 1967 proved to be the undoing of Mendler's brigades in 1973. Tank charges, accompanied by inadequate infantry support, stumbled into concealed Egyptian infantry positions rich in RPG-7 teams and Malyutka missile launchers. After having suffered dreadfully high losses among tank commanders in 1967, Israeli tankers were encouraged to fight 'buttoned up' and so could not easily see the Egyptian anti-tank squads. The Israeli tanks were thrown back with stiff losses. By the afternoon of Sunday 7 October the 252nd Armd. Ugda had been reduced from about 300 to about 100 tanks. By this time the Egyptians had brought across five infantry divisions with their supporting tanks and vehicles, with elements of two armoured divisions and a mechanized infantry division to follow. The Egyptian 2nd Army stretched from the northern banks of the Great Bitter Lake to the Mediterranean, and the 3rd Army stretched from the southern banks to Suez City.

On 7 October the Israelis brought forward two more *ugdas*, the 162nd Reserve Armd. Ugda commanded by Gen. Avraham 'Bren' Adan, and the 143rd Reserve Armd. Ugda commanded by

Gen. Arik Sharon. The battered 252nd Ugda was reorganized and stationed in the south opposite the Egyptian 3rd Army to stop any attacks toward the key Gidi and Mitla Passes. Sharon's command was stationed in the centre opposite the Great Bitter Lake, while Adan's covered the northern area of the Sinai. Adan's 162nd Armd. Ugda consisted of the 460th Armd. Bde. from Mendler's Ugda, which had lost half its strength; the 600th Armd. Bde. under Col. Nathan Baram; and the 217th Armd. Bde. under Col. Arieh Karem. This amounted to about 170 tanks. On 8 October a battalion of the 600th Armd. Bde. attacked the Egyptian 2nd Inf. Div. near Kantara and was nearly wiped out. An attack by the 217th Armd. Bde. against T-54s holding the Chinese Farm also met with heavy losses, and the same fate befell an attack by the 460th Armd. Bde. near Fridan[1]. By the end of the day, Adan's 162nd Ugda was down to only about 120 tanks. It was a dismal day for the Zahal.

On 9 October Sharon's 421st Armd. Bde. made an attack on the southern perimeter of the Chinese Farm, losing 36 tanks. The Egyptians spent the day consolidating positions and began steps to bring the 4th Armd. Div. over to the 3rd Army, and the 21st Armd. Div. over to the 2nd Army. The Israelis moved in the 146th Composite Ugda (Gen. Sasoon) to cover the area north of Kantara and to give Adan's forces more flexibility in dealing with the crisis in the central region. The Israelis anticipated that the Egyptians would eventually try to make a major breakout attempt towards the central Sinai, so rather than continue to impale their tanks on the Egyptian missiles they decided to prepare for this offensive. They rightly guessed that the attack would bring the Egyptians out from underneath their SAM umbrella, and the tank thrusts could be countered both by Israeli tank forces and by air strikes.

The Egyptian attack came on 14 October, with three main armoured punches emanating from 3rd Army positions and three more thrusts from 2nd Army. The Egyptian mechanized columns

[1]The 'Chinese' Farm was a Japanese experimental agricultural station that was the main focus of many battles in the 1973 Sinai campaign. It was overlooked by a hill called 'Missouri' by the Israelis.

quickly shed their infantry support and faced the Israelis in a classic gun-vs-gun duel, where the Israelis had a decided edge both in gunnery training and in equipment. By nightfall the Egyptians had lost 260 tanks and 200 other armoured vehicles, while the Israelis had lost only about 40 tanks. This attack was the largest tank-vs-tank confrontation since the Second World War.

In spite of the very precarious containment of the Egyptian forces the Israelis, especially Gen. Sharon, were itching to snatch the strategic initiative and put a task force on the west bank of the Suez to raise hell in the Egyptian rear areas. The most suitable location was at Deversoir at the northern end of the Great Bitter Lake in a break between the 2nd and 3rd Armies. The Israelis had built hardpoints for bridging areas in this region while they had been in control, and these could be used in the crossing. The main effort would come from Sharon's forces backed up by Adan's tanks. The main stumbling block to the operation was the heavy concentration of Egyptian forces around the Chinese Farm, consisting of the Egyptian 21st Armd. Div. and the

16th Inf. Div. The Israelis underestimated the size of this force, but in the early morning hours of 16 October managed to push a pontoon bridge across the canal unnoticed by the Egyptians. A small contingent of paratroopers with a few tanks were sent across. While this had been going on, Sharon's forces had been fighting a vicious all-night tank battle in an attempt to obtain a secure passage route at the key Akavish–Titur crossroads south of the Chinese Farm. Sharon's units lost about 70 and the Egyptians about 150 tanks in this action. The paratroopers on the west bank were joined by some 175mm M107 self-propelled guns. Attacks were launched by other units on the northern flanks of the 2nd Army to convince the Egyptians that all the commotion near the Akavish–Titur crossroads was just part of an Israeli plan to roll up their flanks. Sharon's losses and the tough Egyptian pressure led the Israelis to bring in Adan's 162nd Ugda to keep the route open. In the afternoon the Egyptians launched a

The Centurion formed the backbone of the Israeli Armoured Corps in 1967 but by 1973 was outnumbered by M48s and M60s. Powerplant and transmission modifications gave the Centurion a new lease of life; the rectangular air cleaner assembly at the rear of the fender identifies this as a modified vehicle.

M109 SP 155mm guns were an important addition to Zahal firepower in 1973. This vehicle's tactical markings are obscured by stowage. After 1973 the M109A1, with better long range performance, was also supplied to Israel.

major counter-attack by two tank brigades on the Akavish–Titur crossroads which went on into the early morning hours of 17 October. The attack was contained by the 460th and 600th Armd. Bdes., and within this small battlefield, 20 kilometres square, the Egyptians lost about 160 tanks and the Israelis about 80. As this engagement was petering out the neighbouring 3rd Army joined the fray by sending 96 T-62s of the 25th Armd. Bde. to help. They were spotted, and the Israeli 14th and 600th Armd. Bdes. laid a hasty ambush. In the slaughter that followed all but ten of the Egyptian tanks were destroyed, and the Israelis lost four tanks in a minefield while pursuing the survivors. This marked the end of any major Egyptian counter-attacked around the Chinese Farm, and the Israelis were able to begin to move forces across the Canal.

The first mission of the forces on the west bank was to silence the Egyptian missile batteries so that the Israeli Air Force could attack the Egyptian bridgehead on the east bank. The M107s struck the nearest site, and tank forays fanned out to eliminate others. On the night of 17–18 October Adan's 162nd Ugda moved across the bridges at Deversoir with 200 tanks of the 217th, 460th and 600th Armd. Bdes. These forces were later joined by Magen's 252nd Ugda[1], and the 14th and 421st Armd. Bdes. of Sharon's

[1]Gen. Kalman Magen took command of the 252nd Ugda after Gen. Albert Mendler was killed when his command vehicle suffered a direct artillery hit.

143rd Ugda. Adan's and Magen's Ugdas spread out southward to cut off the supplies of the 3rd Army, while Sharon's forces moved northward towards Ismalia.

The Egyptians made desperate attempts to destroy the bridges at Deversoir, and when this failed efforts were made to secure a ceasefire through UN mediation. The United States and the Soviet Union became embroiled in a major political confrontation; but as the superpowers both favoured a ceasefire, one was attempted on the night of 22–23 October. It quickly failed due to the confused situation on the west bank, and the Israelis made a last-ditch drive towards Suez City to completely cut off the 3rd Army. An attack into Suez City itself was bloodily repulsed, and on 24 October the second ceasefire came into effect. There were a number of outbreaks of fighting subsequent to the ceasefire before UNEF forces were able to establish a buffer zone. Through UN mediation the fragile ceasefire held intact; and in January 1974 the Israelis agreed to withdraw their forces from the west bank under UN supervision, and a UN buffer force was established.

The 1973 war, unlike the previous Middle East wars, did not end in a clearcut victory for either side. The Egyptian Army succeeded in obtaining Sadat's political objective of ending the deadlocked negotiations over the fate of the Sinai, and in the process redeemed the image of the Egyptian Army, so badly tarnished by the humiliating routs of 1956 and 1967. Much of the credit can be claimed by the tenacious Egyptian infantrymen who so determindly fought back the initial Israeli tank attacks. Nevertheless, Egyptian soldiers had been quite stubborn in defensive operations in past wars; the real contrast between 1973 and the previous wars was the quality of Egyptian leadership. Although Zahal did not win as sweeping a victory in 1973 as it had in 1967, any doubts about its hard-earned reputation were laid to rest by the amazing defence of the Golan Heights in the critical early days of the war, and by the adventurous and skilled crossing of the Suez Canal. Overcoming the complacency which had led to the early defeats, Zahal quickly adapted to the new tactics and prosecuted a difficult two-front war against enemy forces which heavily outnumbered it in men and equipment. The Syrian Army failed in its objectives, though many Syrian tank units displayed a great deal more skill than in 1967.

★ ★ ★

Few of the wars in the Middle East had such dramatic repercussions in the armies outside the region as did the 1973 October War. Uninformed journalists claimed to see in this war 'the end of the tank'. In fact, the early defeats of Israeli armour by Arab anti-tank missile teams only served to reinforce traditional NATO and Warsaw Pact doctrine regarding the need for an integrated combined arms team. The Israelis quickly appreciated the differences between 1973 and 1967, and began to mix more mechanized infantry into their tank formations. The main disadvantage of a missile like the Sagger is that it must be carefully guided all along its slow flight path. The Israelis found that by spraying the area around the Malyutka launcher with machine gun fire the moment they became aware the missile had been launched, the operator could be forced to duck and the missile would pass harmlessly overhead. Suppressive fire from infantry half-tracks and M113s, combined with mortar and artillery support, greatly reduced Israeli tank casualties to the missiles.

Experiences with the missiles also greatly accelerated the deployment of new composite (Chobham) armour that had been under development since the 1950s. This new armour, using conventional steel with layers of non-metallic plate, is completely invulnerable to the type of shaped charges used in small anti-tank missiles like the Malyutka and RPG-7. Armour of this type is now being used on tanks such as the US M1 Abrams, the Leopard II, the British Challenger and MBT-80 and the Soviet T-80.

The Middle East wars have served as testing grounds for the weapons of the superpowers. Without generous outside support the countries of the Middle East, whose modest economies are smaller than those of many European and American cities, certainly could not afford to wage a war on as lavish a scale as that of 1973. The lessons learned in these wars have been quickly incorporated into the training manuals and design studies of the armies of NATO and the Warsaw Pact.

Among the Israeli tanks, the Centurion with its many Israeli modifications proved to be a popular and solid performer. The same could be said for the M48, though the performance of the M60A1 revealed some serious problems. American tanks have very fast turret traverse made

Syrian T-55s and BMP infantry combat vehicle of the force which broke through Israeli lines at Rafid during fighting with the 188th Barak Armd. Bde. in October 1973. The tanks, painted in the three-tone scheme, have infra-red searchlights—these gave Syrian tankers a decided advantage in night combat with the overtaxed Israeli defenders.

pelled guns, which were able to counter the numerical superiority of Arab artillery by their great mobility.

The Soviet equipment used by the Syrians and Egyptians had its share of vices and virtues. The T-55 and T-62 are both simpler and less expensive than their Western counterparts, and because of their lower cost more were available. Their principal advantages aside from quantity were their low profile and good armour. Their fire control systems, which rely on primitive stadiametric ranging, were adequate at short range, but performed poorly in long-range duels. The 115mm gun of the T-62 proved to be especially effective, but the poor interior layout of the vehicle and its cramped design led to poor 'habitability' and degraded the performance of the overworked crew during long battles. Their excellent armour was compromised by the vulnerable positioning of internal fuel and ammunition supplies, and the Israelis have said that some tanks suffered from internal detonation of these stores even from glancing hits that did not penetrate the thick armour. The BMP proved to be both fast and well-armed compared to previous armoured troop carriers. Its main gun, which relies on a rocket developed from the RPG-7, is accurate only in still air, and aiming the Malyutka missile from a moving troop carrier did not prove to be very effective. The rear firing ports proved ineffective due to the cramped interior and rocky ride, and like all APCs the BMP is quite thinly armoured and vulnerable to heavy machine gun fire at the sides and rear.

The Lebanese Civil War

Although Lebanon managed to escape involvement in most of the conflicts in the Middle East, the use of southern Lebanon by the PLO as a staging area for raids into Israel, coupled with the inevitable Israeli reprisals, destabilized this

possible by an elaborate hydraulic system. Unfortunately, the system used in the M60A1 sprayed a fine mist of hydraulic fluid into the fighting compartment when ruptured by a hit; because of its low flashpoint this quickly exploded, seriously burning the crew. This was quickly remedied after the war.

One of the most serious deficiencies of Israeli tanks was their lack of night-vision systems. The Syrian and Egyptian tanks were amply equipped with infra-red systems; in many night encounters this put the Israelis at a serious disadvantage, and was a major contributory cause to the high losses on the Golan Heights in the first nights of the war. After the war the Israelis began acquiring sophisticated image-intensification and thermal-imaging night vision systems, which are superior to the older infra-red systems since they do not require a detectable searchlight but are able to operate by sensing ambient starlight and thermal emissions.

The M113 was a popular successor to the old half-tracks, and was affectionately called 'Zelda'. Probably the most successful armoured vehicles of the war were the M107 and M109 self-pro-

fragile nation. Made up of both Christian and Moslem Arabs in a tenuous balance, the country split along religious lines in the civil war which broke out in 1975. The Christians flocked to the militias organized by the Falangist Party, while the Moslems joined PLO groups or formed groups of their own. The Lebanese Army disintegrated and its armoured vehicles, consisting of M41s, M42 Dusters, AMX-13s, Charioteers, M113s and an assortment of armoured cars, fell into the hands of the competing militias. The Falangists received Israeli support and some groups in southern Lebanon received some old M50 Super-Shermans and some M113s, while the PLO received some vehicles from Syria. Both factions tried with some success to buy arms on the international black market, including a varied assortment of V-150 Commando armoured cars, M113s and AML-90 armoured cars. United Nations efforts restored a kind of peace, though the Syrian, French and other peace-keeping units have been involved in sporadic outbreaks with the various militias.

Colours and Markings

Where it has been possible to study actual paint chips reference is given here in a five-digit code based on American Federal Standard (FS 595 A) followed by the three-digit code from the *Methuen Handbook of Colour*. For obvious reasons these are approximate matches only. For markings, see particularly plates D and F.

Israel
The early 'sandwich armour' trucks were painted sand yellow, with a white band painted horizontally all round the front, rear and sides. Most vehicles obtained in 1948 were in olive drab, of either the American variety (Federal Standard 34087/Methuen 4F7) or the greener British version. Israeli modified armoured cars seem to have been painted a similar colour. Initially

markings were limited to chalked Hebrew names and slogans; later some standardized markings appeared. Southern Command vehicles used three white arrows stacked horizontally; another command used a single arrow. The AFVs of Sadeh's 8th Armd. Bde. used two white diagonal bars on turret or hull sides. Both four-digit serial numbers, and large white three-digit tactical numbers were allotted, but the allocation system is not clear. Many vehicles were unmarked.

Many AFVs retained a plain appearance after the war. New acquisitions from France retained the French Army version of olive drab, which faded to a brownish 'field drab'. Military serials were introduced to hull front and rear positions, and often there was a separate serial for the turret. Serials were white, often on black backgrounds, and had as a suffix or prefix the Hebrew character *tsadi*, the first letter of the word *Zahal*. Around 1956 a bridging sign was introduced, a blue disc edged red bearing the vehicle weight classification in white. For Operation 'Kadesh' air recognition markings were painted on tank rear engine decks in the form of a large blue 'X' edged white or on a white disc; on other vehicle types it was painted on the bonnet. Tank turrets sometimes bore a white 'X', and the same sign was hastily applied to 'captures' pressed into service. AMX-13s carried the marking on the turret roof or the circular spare roadwheel cover.

The 1956 war emphasized the need for better tactical markings. The style adopted had four basic elements. On the turret were a Hebrew letter and a number, indicating the individual tank and the platoon respectively; since platoons

The Syrian attack on the Israeli 'Purple Line' was spearheaded by engineers with PT-54 mine-rolling tanks to breach Israeli minefields. This example, used in 1974 to clear mines from the UN buffer zone on the Golan Heights, is painted plain Soviet dark green; in 1973 many Syrian AFVs were camouflaged. (United Nations: Y. Nagata)

T-62 of the Egyptian 4th Armd. Div. near El Kabrit during UN-sponsored disengagement of forces in February 1974. The Yom Kippur war left large Israeli forces on the west bank of the Canal behind the Egyptian 3rd Army; following negotiations they were pulled back into the Sinai, and Egyptian forces like these took their place. (United Nations: Y. Nagata)

were seldom larger than three tanks the first three letters in the Hebrew alphabet were used: *aleph*, *beth* and *gimel*. From one to four white stripes were painted round the gun barrel to indicate the company. A large white chevron was painted on the hull or turret side.

The meaning of the chevron is open to debate. The theory that it is a battalion sign is unlikely to be true since photos show several different chevrons on tanks clearly of a single battalion. Statistical correlation of photos of Israeli tanks in 1960–67 suggests a link between chevron direction and number of barrel-bands. In the author's belief the chevrons are company markings, like the barrel-bands; but it is possible the chevrons were used as battalion signs in 1973. The system appears to have been: chevron downwards = 1st Coy., chevron forwards = 2nd Coy., chevron upwards = 3rd Coy., chevron backwards = 4th Coy. or HQ section. Numerous exceptions to this system shown in photos suggest varying use of the symbols from brigade to brigade, but it is believed that the system described was the most common.

The turret number and letter were often painted on a removable panel, probably allowing crews to train with a single call-sign, moving the panel to whichever tank they were assigned.

Prior to the 1967 war Zahal replaced olive drab paint with 'sand grey' (36350/5E3), most Israeli tanks being repainted in this shade before the outbreak of war. Tanks carried fluorescent panels for air identification, but half-tracks, trucks and some tanks had a central white band edged black painted down the centre-line of the top surfaces; half-tracks had this on the vertical rear hull plates and on the bonnet, ending at the front in a T-bar out over the wings. On tanks it was not common, and was usually confined to turret roofs.

Many Israeli units had 'heraldic' brigade insignia, which were applied only for peacetime parades and were not used in combat. Some unit insignia were used in the 1967 war but in most cases their meaning is unknown. The 79th Tank Bn. of 7th Armd. Bde. painted the letter *aleph* on the fender as a battalion sign, and this may have related to the first letter of the battalion CO's name—Elad.

Markings in 1973 were much as in 1967, although, as mentioned, tank brigade re-organization may have led to the use of the chevrons as battalion signs. There was a distinct increase in the number of tactical insignia painted on the fenders, a selection of which are shown on Plate F, but their meaning is unknown. There is reason to believe that some were brigade or divisional markings assigned for the duration of the campaign. Some tanks and APCs bore company stripes and turret letters repeated on the rear of the hull, the stripes being marked horizontally to the upper right of the Hebrew letter. Many vehicles did not carry complete sets of markings, but only one or two of the basic signs. In view of the harried state of Zahal in the 1973 war this is hardly surprising.

Egypt

From minimal photographic evidence, it would appear that Egyptian tanks in the late 1940s were painted either desert sand or olive drab and bore very few markings. A Mk VI light tank disabled at Yad Mordechai in 1948 had a large white '32' painted on the turret side; and some armoured cars bore British-style squadron signs on the turret. Bren carriers commonly carried a green/white/green roundel.

When the 4th Armd. Div. was formed after 1954 some vehicles bore 'heraldic' insignia, possibly indicating battalions, for parade purposes. These included a mounted spearman; a prowling tiger (both T-34/85s); a diving hawk (SU-100); and a spread eagle (IS-3M Stalin). (See Plate D, and also *Vanguard 14, The T-34 Tank.*) The SU-100s of the 53rd Arty. Bty. encountered at Port Said in 1956 bore a green and white crescent marking (see Plate D), and other Egyptian vehicles at this time still bore British-style squadron signs. The great majority were unmarked and were simply painted overall light sand. Some tanks carried a small rectangular red and light blue flash forward on the turret sides; this does not appear to be a divisional sign and from its widespread use may have been a form of national or branch insignia.

Following the 1956 war Egyptian armour was more often marked with three-digit turret numbers in black Arabic characters. Even compared to the very limited use of markings in 1956, Egyptian tanks in 1967 were exceptionally plain and normally unmarked. During the 1973 war sprayed camouflage painting was more evident, usually in medium brown in a wide variety of patterns. In this campaign a variety of turret bands and bars were also seen in conjunction with three-digit numbers, but there is no information available on their meaning.

Syria

There is an almost complete lack of photographic evidence on Syrian armour in 1948; available photos show no markings, though some captured Syrian R-35s still bore French serial numbers and thus were presumably still finished in French Army green.

Tanks used in 1967 were uniformly painted dark green, either Soviet (34098/4F5) or from local stock. Names were frequently painted on turret sides in white Arabic script, often referring to heroes of past wars, including the 1948 campaign. A thick white ring was painted on turret roofs as air identification. Examples are known of geometrical symbols painted, often in red, on turret sides (see *Vanguard 14, The T-34 Tank*). The glacis often bore a white five-digit Arabic serial and the name 'Al-Jaish' ('Army').

In 1973 the Syrians adopted standard Soviet desert camouflage of olive green with large blotches of sand yellow (30257/5D5), and some-

The scourge of Israeli tanks in 1973—the deadly little 9M14M Malyutka wire-guided AT missile. The missile was launched from its 'suitcase' container (left) while the operator controlled it using the sight and 'joystick' (right). To hit a tank with a device like this under combat conditions requires considerable practice and nerve. (James Loop)

times with additional blotches of medium grey.

Three-digit turret numbers generally replaced the turret names, painted in white and presumably indicating company/platoon/vehicle; in some units these were contained within a thin white 'box' with solid or broken edges. Some vehicles bore a white disc with a coloured triangle on the turret roof, presumably as air identification. With the formation of armoured divisions, divisional insignia were adopted; these were usually painted forward on the turret sides, and off-set to one side of the glacis and rear plate. These consisted of a white rectangular outline round a pair of coloured geometric shapes; the sequence is not known, but examples are shown on Plates D and G.

Jordan

Jordanian armour has traditionally followed British marking practice, with some variation. The armoured cars of the Arab Legion in 1948 were often left unmarked, painted in overall sand. For parades, at least, they often bore British squadron signs on the turrets, and sometimes a hawk insignia on the bow plates. During the early days of the Armoured Corps in the 1950s regimental badges were adopted for the 1st and 2nd Armd. Car Regts. and the 3rd Tank Regt., and these are seen in photos of formal parades, at least: yellow panels bearing a green wreath and red crown with the motifs of crossed lances, a

Egyptian PT-54 mine-roller clearing paths in the UN's Sinai buffer zone in March 1974. It is painted in the usual sand and drab brown camouflage. Many Egyptian tanks in 1973 bore two white stripes painted down the edges of the front fenders, as here; the significance is uncertain. (United Nations)

The Plates

hawk's head, and a scorpion respectively. In 1967 most armour was painted earth yellow (30257/5D6) with olive drab stripes (34087/4F7) sprayed on in a diagonal wavy pattern. Some Centurions displayed dark blue-grey in place of olive drab. Markings included an arm of service square on the left front fender as viewed, red and yellow for the 40th and red and blue for the 60th Armd. Bdes.; the number of the brigade was normally painted in white on these squares. On the right fender as viewed a black panel bore a white serial number below the word 'Al-Jaish'. Turret names were common, and from photos seem to have been either those of historical or recent heroes or royal personages. Most tanks bore British squadron signs on the turrets, but it is not certain if these followed British sequence exactly. If they did, then they were a triangle for 'A' Sqn., a square for 'B', a circle for 'C', and a diamond for HQ. The British colour sequence was red for the senior battalion in a brigade, yellow for the second, and blue and green for the third and fourth, though the smaller Jordanian brigades presumably did not follow this sequence through. In the post-1970 period Jordanian armour went over to a three-tone pattern of camouflage: sand (30277), earth red (30117) and olive (34087).

A1: *Hotchkiss H-39, 'Russian Company', 82nd Tank Battalion, Israeli 8th Armoured Brigade; Lydda airport, 1948*
Crewed by volunteers who had served in armoured units in Eastern Europe in the Second World War, mainly Russian and Polish Jews, this 'company' had a few H-39s still in faded French olive green paint. White diagonals indicate the brigade; behind them is the number '421', and a Zahal serial '3989' is painted on the hull.

A2: *Marmon-Herrington Mk IVF of an independent armoured car company, Arab Legion; Palestine, 1948*
Arab Legion armoured cars were either left in overall sand colour, or over-sprayed with a wavy olive drab pattern, as here. Blue British-style 'A' Sqn. marking on turret side may not have same meaning as in British service. Stylized hawk's head unit insignia on bow plate; British serial below driver's position; Arab Legion number '851' on right fender, as viewed. This was sometimes repeated on the other fender in Western script.

B1: *M9 half-track with modified British 6pdr. AT gun, 82nd Tank Bn., Israeli 8th Armd. Bde.; Negev, 1948*

Note raised and plated-over driver's position, and MG .34 mounted beside him. Zahal serial '3282', vehicle's tactical number '332', three arrows of Southern Command, and two diagonals of 8th Armd. Bde. all painted in white on original olive drab.

B2: *Archer SP 17pdr., Egyptian independent anti-tank company; Sinai campaign, 1956*

Most such vehicles were painted plain sand all over; one of the four companies used this green and white roundel national insignia in six positions.

B3: *White M3A1 Scout Car, Israeli Military Border Police, 1954*

Original overall olive drab, with Border Police insignia on hull side in white. The significance of the fender insignia is not known. Unlike the Army, the Border Police wear British-style battle-dress and ranking, and green berets. Subsequent to the 1967 war the Police BTR-152s and Walids were painted dark green with the flower-like insignia on the hull sides in a comparable position.

C1: *M1 Sherman (M4A1 76mm, wet stowage), Israeli 7th Armoured Brigade; Operation 'Kadesh', Sinai, 1956*

Overall olive drab faded to a brownish shade, with the 1956–57 blue and white Israeli air identification cross. White-on-black Zahal serial blocks on hull sides and mantlet. Some Shermans of the 27th Armd. Bde. bore white 'X's hastily painted on the turret sides.

C2: *AMX-13, 2ᵉ Régiment Etranger de Cavalerie attaché 1ᵉʳ Régiment Etranger Parachutiste; Port Said, 1956*

French and British vehicles employed in Operation 'Musketeer' had a hasty coat of sand yellow overall, with a horizontal black stripe painted round the turret as a recognition sign, and a white 'H' (for 'Hamilcar', the original codename for the operation) as an air identification sign on the roof. The only other marking is the usual French *matricule* in white digits with a tricolour flash on black strips on the front and rear hull. The Foreign Legion cavalry in Algeria, from

During the Lebanese civil war Israeli forces frequently crossed the border in reprisal for PLO raids. In 1978 Israel agreed to withdraw from southern Lebanon, to be replaced by a UNEF military buffer force. Here a heavily armed M3 half-track and a modified Centurion, typical of Israeli vehicles with their plethora of stowage and gear, prepare to move back into Israel. (United Nations: Zuhair Saade)

The Lebanese civil war was brought to a forcible halt in 1978 by the arrival of UNIFIL Interim Forces and Syrian troops. This Syrian BTR-152 V2, painted overall dark green and marked '1358', was photographed patrolling Saida in March 1978. (United Nations: J. K. Isaac)

which this squadron was detached, did not at this date wear the green beret and camouflage suit, which appear to have been issued by the paras to whom they were attached for the Suez campaign.

D1: *T-55, unit unknown, Egyptian Army; Sinai, 1967*
The turret digits appear to indicate service with the 3rd Platoon of a tank company, but the black bars are unexplained.

D2: *PzKpfw IV Ausf.H of an independent tank battalion, Syrian Army; Golan Heights, 1967*
This tank was assigned to one of the independent battalions supporting infantry brigades, but exact allocation is unknown. The usual Syrian overall dark green is relieved only by a white ring on the turret roof, and by the white turret name 'Suleiman', referring to a hero of some past war.

Arab Insignia

(A1–A10)	Arabic numerals 1–10 in the normal form seen on vehicles.
(E1)	Large hull marking borne by SU-100s, Egyptian 53rd Arty. Bty., 4th Armd. Div., Port Said, 1956.
(E2, E3, E5)	Parade insignia used in Egyptian 4th Armd. Div., respectively on T-34/85, SU-100 and IS-3M Stalin.
(E4)	National insignia very occasionally seen on Egyptian tanks during the short life of the 'United Arab Republic'.
(E6)	Insignia widely seen on Egyptian tanks in 1967, usually low and forward on turret sides; significance unknown.
(J1)	Jordanian 2nd Armd. Car Regt., 1950s, usually on bow plate.
(J2)	Jordanian 1st Armd. Car Regt., 1950s.
(J3)	Jordanian 40th Armd. Bde., 1967.
(J4)	Jordanian 60th Armd. Bde., 1967.
(J5)	Usual style of 'Al-Jaish' plate on Syrian (top) and Jordanian (bottom) tanks.
(J6)	Insignia of a Jordan Arab Legion independent armoured car company, 1948.
(J7)	Jordanian 8th Royal Artillery Bn. (attached 40th Armd. Bde.) post-1967.
(J8)	Jordanian 40th Armd. Bde., post-1967.
(J9)	Jordanian 60th Armd. Bde., post-1967.
(J10)	Jordanian artillery bn. attached 60th Armd. Bde., post-1967.
(S1)	Syrian air identification insignia used on some tank turret roofs, forward; 1973.
(S2, S3)	Syrian tank brigade insignia, 1970-73, carried on turret sides or hull front and rear.
(S4)	Syrian air identification sign used in 1967 on tank turret roofs, forward.
(S5, S6)	Syrian unit insignia carried by BRDM recce platoons.

E1: *M48A2C Patton, 2nd Platoon, 2nd Company, 79th Tank Bn., Israeli 7th Armd. Bde., Ugda Tal; Sinai, 1967*
Overall 'sand grey' with company chevron on turret side, and battalion insignia, the character *aleph*, on right rear fender—this was also seen on front right fender, as viewed. Vehicle and platoon insignia, *Aleph-2*, on removable canvas panel. Signal flags were often used by Israeli tank commanders.

E2: *M47 Patton, Jordanian 40th Armd. Bde.; West Bank, 1967*
British-style red triangle on turret may suggest

'A' Sqn. of this brigade's 2nd Tank Bn., but cannot be positively identified. Usual earth yellow and olive camouflage; brigade insignia on left front fender as viewed, and serial '11521' below 'Al-Jaish' on right fender. The black Arabic script turret name is 'Al-Hussein'.

F1: *M48 Patton, Jordanian 60th Armd. Bde.; West Bank, 1967*
Similar camouflage and markings to previous tank; brigade insignia on fender would be as shown for this formation on Plate D, and turret sign suggests 'C' Sqn. of its battalion. Turret name is 'Abu Abaida', a warrior hero of the 7th century.

F2: *M7 Priest 105mm SP of an Israeli independent artillery battalion; Sinai, 1967*
Standard 'sand grey'. The chevron presumably indicates the battery within the battalion, and the number '4' may indicate the troop within the battery.

Israeli Insignia

(1–4) Standard tactical insignia, discussed in text.
(5) Hebrew character *aleph*, sometimes painted resembling Roman 'N'.
(6) Hebrew character *beth*.
(7) Hebrew character *gimel*.
(8) Occasionally seen on command half-tracks, 1967, and may have been an HQ symbol in some units.
(9) Sometimes painted on captured Soviet tanks in 1973 to avoid identification as Syrian or Egyptian.
(10) Company barrel markings for 1st to 4th Coys., as discussed in text.
(11) Southern Command, 1948, Negev and Sinai.
(12) 8th Armd. Bde., 1948.
(13) One style of bridge plate; unbroken red ring touching blue disc also common.
(14) An armoured brigade insignia, 1957.
(15) Parade insignia, 7th Armd. Bde.
(16) Unidentified Israeli Staghound armoured car unit, 1950s.

Apart from the red Star of David, which is the Israeli equivalent of the red cross marked on

Among the UNIFIL peacekeeping forces in Lebanon was a French paratroop detachment supported by several AML-60-7 armoured cars. Photographed south of the Litani River near Tyre, this AML displays typical white paint scheme with black or dark blue UN markings. (United Nations: J. K. Isaac)

ambulance vehicles, all other insignia illustrated are unit or formation tactical insignia seen on Israeli tanks, 1967 and 1973. Some presumably identify brigades, and others whole divisional task forces.

G1: *M113A1, Falangist militia; Beirut, 1975*
Most Falangist APCs were acquired from Lebanese Army stock or handed over by Israel, and were left in plain sand overall; some sported more garish schemes, such as olive or grey striping and spotting, or this green, black and rust pattern. The Lebanese national insignia is reproduced on the engine compartment cover; other vehicles had large religious pictures applied. An ACAV kit is fitted over the .50 cal. MG mounting.

G2: *T-62A of unidentified Syrian armoured brigade; Golan Heights, 1973*
Overall Soviet green oversprayed with sand and medium grey. Three-digit turret number '536' presumably indicates vehicle, platoon and company, but sequence is not confirmed. On the glacis and hull rear the Syrian serial and 'Al-Jaish' appear above a brigade insignia; many combinations of these coloured geometric symbols are known, but the meaning is unexplained.

H1: *M50 Super-Sherman, Falangist militia; southern Lebanon, 1977*
Handed over by the Israelis to the Christian

Lebanese groups who guard the border zone against PLO incursion, these old Shermans are often painted in grey with green stripes; insignia are limited to the Lebanese flag, and in some cases a crudely painted cross or 'X' on the turret sides.

H2: *T-62, Egyptian 4th Armd. Div.; Sinai, 1973*
Overall light sand with 'field drab' brown camouflage; examples are known of both this soft-edged sprayed version, and of hard-edged hand-painted camouflage. The turret number '431' suggests possible identification as command tank, 3rd Platoon, 4th Company. The small rough area of white paint ahead of this suggests that an insignia has been painted out.

H3: *Charioteer tank destroyer, PLO; southern Lebanon, 1976*
This is one of the elderly vehicles originally sold by Britain to Jordan for use by the 3rd Tank Regt.; subsequently sold to Lebanon when Jordan received Centurions, it was one of several acquired by the PLO during the disintegration of the Lebanese Army in the civil war. This particular vehicle was later knocked out by the Israelis during fighting in southern Lebanon; forward on the turret sides it carries the Moslem greeting and rallying-cry 'Allahu Akhbar', 'God is Great'.

Farbtafeln

A1: Hotchkiss H-39s benutzt bei *Zahal* waren in der originalen französisch grünen Farbe: die weissen diagonalen Streifen lassen die 8th Brigade erkennen, die Nummern bezeichnen den individuellen Panzer. **A2:** Das 'A' Squadron Zeichen im britischen Stil, mag nicht genau dieselbe Bedeutung wie im britischen Dienst zu haben. Arabische Nummer '851' auf dem rechten vorderen Rumpf.

B1: Überdachter Fahrersitz und Maschinengewehr installiert. Das Drei-Pfeile-Zeichen identifiziert das *Zahal* südliche Kommando. **B2:** Die meisten dieser Fahrzeuge waren ganz in einfacher Sandfarbe gestrichen; eine der vier Kompanien benutzte dieses Kokardezeichen. **B3:** Das wie eine Blume geformte Zeichen auf der Wannenseite ist das der Grenzpolizei; das Zeichen auf dem vorderen Kettenschutz ist nicht identifiziert. Die Grenzpolizei benutzt Uniformen im britischen Stil und grüne Baskenmützen.

C1: Die original französische Farbzusammenstellung, ausgeblichen zu einem braunen Farbton. Die einzigen zu dieser Zeit benutzten Markierungen waren das blaue Kreuz zur Erkennung für die israelischen Flugzeuge und die Seriennummern am Rumpf und Turm. **C2:** Alle französischen und britischen Panzer in Operation 'Musketier' trugen einen schwarzen Erkennungsstreifen rund um den Turm und ein weisses 'H' auf dem Dach zur Erkennung durch Flugzeuge.

D1: Die Turmnummern scheinen den Dienst mit dem 3. Zug zu kennzeichnen, die schwarzen Streifen sind jedoch unerklärt. **D2:** Nicht sichtbar ist hier eine weisse Ringmarkierung auf dem Turmdach—Siehe S4 unten; der Turmname ist 'Suleiman'. **D3:** Siehe Untertitel in engl. Sprache, die im Grossen und Ganzen selbsterklärend sind.

E1: Israelische Farbe, bekannt als 'sandgrau'. Man glaubt, dass der Armwinkel zu dieser Zeit die 2. Kompanie erkennen liess; die Turmnummer 'Aleph-2' auf einem Leinwandstück lässt den 2. Zug, erster Panzer erkennen; und das Schriftzeichen *Aleph* auf dem hinteren Rumpf rechts wurde als Bataillonszeichen benutzt. **E2:** Die Turminschrift ist ein im britischen Stil gehaltenes 'A' Schwadronen Dreieck und der arabische Name 'Al-Hussein'. Das Brigadezeichen am vorderen Rumpf links; Seriennummer und 'Al-Jaish'—'Army' am vorderen Rumpf, rechts.

F1: Wiederum Turminschrift ähnlich der im britischen Stil gehaltenen 'C' Schwadronen Markierung. Der Turmname ist 'Abu Abaida', ein Kriegsheld des 7. Jahrhunderts. Brigadenmarkierung wie in Bildtafel D, Abschnitt J4. **F2:** Das Armwinkelzeichen lässt vermutlich die Batterie innerhalb des Bataillons erkennen; die '4' zeigt vermutlich den Zug innerhalb der Batterie an. **F3:** Siehe Untertitel im Grossen und Ganzen selbsterklärend sind. Gegenstände 1–4 wurden im Jahr 1967 benutzt, um die 1. bis 4. Kompanie innerhalb eines Bataillons erkennbar zu machen, jedoch mögen sie im Jahr 1973, zu mindest in manchen Fällen, das Bataillon innerhalb einer Brigade angezeigt haben.

G1: Typische auffallende Farbzusammenstellung dieser irregulären Militz; andere M113s waren sandfarben, übermalt mit grünen oder grauen Streifen und Punkten und grossen religiösen Bildern, die auf der Aussenseite des Fahrzeuges aufgeklebt waren! **G2:** Sowietische Wüstentarnung in grün, übersprüht mit sandgelben und grauen Flecken. Die bunten Formen zeigen eine Brigade an, sind jedoch nicht identifiziert.

H1: Ein primitiv gemaltes Kreuz oder 'X' ist die einzige Markierung, die normalerweise getragen wurde; der libanesische Flaggenentwurf ist wie Bildtafel G1. **H2:** Beispiele sind zu sehen, sowohl mit der 'weichen' gesprühten Tarnungsfarbe, als auch mit der 'harten' handgemalten Streifen. Turmnummer '431'. **H3:** Vormals benutzt von jordanischen und libanesischen Armeen, einige dieser alten Fahrzeuge wurden von der PLO erworben. Der Wahlspruch auf dem Turm ist 'Allahu Akhbar!'

Notes sur les planches en couleur

A1: Les Hotchkiss H-39 utilisés par *Zahal* étaient peints dans les couleurs françaises originales; les raies diagonales blanches identifient la 8e Brigade, les nombres indiquent le numéro individuel du char. **A2:** Le signe 'A' Squadron sur la tourelle n'avait peut-être pas exactement la même signification que dans l'armée anglaise. Sur le devant de la caisse, à droite, le nombre 851 en arabe.

B1: La position du pilote avait été munie d'un toit, et une mitrailleuse avait été installée. L'insigne des trois flèches identifie la région militaire du Sud de *Zahal*. **B2:** La plupart de ces véhicules étaient peints entièrement couleur sable; l'une des quatre compagnies utilisait cette cocarde comme insigne. **B3:** L'insigne en forme de fleur sur le côté de la caisse est celui de la police de la région frontière; l'insigne sur le garde-boue avant n'a pas été identifié. La police de la frontière porte un uniforme de style anglais, avec béret vert.

C1: La couleur olive française originale était décolorée au ton brun. Les seules marques utilisées à ce moment là étaient la croix bleue pour permettre de les faire reconnaître par l'aviation israélienne, et les numéros de série sur la caisse et sur la tourelle. **C2:** Tous les chars française et anglais de l'opération 'Mousquetaire' portaient une bande noire d'identification tout autour de la tourelle, et un 'H' blanc sur le toit de façon à être reconnus par l'aviation.

D1: Les nombres sur les tourelles semblent indiquer service dans le troisième peloton, mais les raies noires sont inexpliquées. **D2:** Invisible ici, il y a un cercle blanc sur le toit de la tourelle—voir S4, ci-dessous; le nom de la tourelle est 'Suleiman'. **D3:** Voir les sous-titres anglais qui se passent en général d'explications.

E1: Ce ton de peinture israélienne était connu sous le nom de 'gris-sable'. Alors le chevron paraissait identifier la deuxième compagnie; le nombre de la tourelle 'Aleph-2' sur le panneau de toile identifiait le deuxième peloton, premier char; et le caractère *aleph*, à l'arrière de la caisse, sur la droite, était utilisé comme insigne de bataillon. **E2:** L'insigne en triangle de la tourelle est celui de l'éscadron 'A'—style anglais—et le nom arabe est 'Al Hussein'. Sur la caisse, devant, à gauche, l'insigne de la brigade; le numéro de série et 'Al Jaish'—'Armée'—sur la caisse, devant, à droite.

F1: De nouveau, insigne de tourelle similaire à celui de l'éscadron 'C', style anglais. Le nom sur la tourelle est 'Abu Abaida', un héro guerrier du septième siècle. Marque de brigade comme plaque D, numéro J4. **F2:** On présume que l'insigne du chevron identifie la batterie du bataillon; '4' indique sans doute le peloton de la batterie. **F3:** Voir les sous-titres anglais qui se passent en général d'explications. Les numéros de 1 à 4 étaient utilisés pour identifier les compagnies du bataillon en 1967, mais ils peuvent avoir servis à identifier les bataillons d'une brigade en 1973, au moins dans quelques cas.

G1: Ces tons flamboyants étaient typiques de cette milice irrégulière; d'autres M113 avaient été peints couleur sable par dessus avec des bandes et des points verts ou gris, ainsi que de grandes images religieuses collées sur l'extérieur du véhicule. **G2:** Camouflage russe du désert, en vert avec des taches jaune-sable et grises. Les formes en couleur indiquent une brigade, mais n'ont pas été identifiées.

H1: La croix peinte sommairement, ou un 'X' est la seule marque portée; le dessin du drapeau libanais est comme sur la plaque G1. **H2:** Des exemples peuvent être vus soit avec les tons légers du camouflage au pistolet, soit avec les bandes criardes peintes à la main. Numéro de tourelle '431'. **H3:** Autrefois utilisé par les armées du Liban et de la Jordanie, quelques une de ces vieux véhicules avaient été acquis par le FPLP. Le slogan sur la tourelle est 'Allahu Akhbar.'